PRAISE FOR *THE FALSE PROMISE OF BIG GOVERNMENT*

"A powerful critique of the central premise behind most efforts to increase the size of government. Garry's argument is full of surprising and sometimes shocking evidence. It is timely and uncompromising."
   —**Robert F. Nagel**, Rothgerber Professor of Constitutional Law at the University of Colorado Law School

"Garry explodes the most treasured myth of the behemoth of modern American government—that whatever stray inefficiencies it may display, it at least benefits the poor. Not so, he lucidly shows. Contrary to the rhetoric that has advanced the expansion of government, the most egalitarian antipoverty program we could have is a drastic reduction in the size of government."
   —**Matthew J. Franck**, director of the Witherspoon Institute's Simon Center on Religion and the Constitution

"Patrick Garry has a gift for making sophisticated ideas accessible to lawyers and nonlawyers alike. In *The False Promise of Big Government*, he brilliantly argues that big government rewards the rich and the powerful at the expense of the average person. This is an important book that should be widely read."
   —**Richard Duncan**, professor of law at the University of Nebraska

"In this readable volume, Garry convincingly demonstrates that governmental regulations and programs too often reinforce the status quo and serve the interests of the wealthy and politically connected. This book belongs on the shelf of anyone interested in the role of government in American life today."
   —**James W. Ely Jr.**, professor emeritus of law and history at Vanderbilt University

"Garry provides a clear-eyed analysis of the myriad ways in which government programs designed to help the poor and struggling actually do far more harm than good. Both compelling and compassionate, *The False Promise of Big Government* offers a searing indictment of our current War on Poverty. One cannot read this book without believing that we can do better."
   —**Michael Tanner**, senior fellow at the Cato Institute

"In this important and timely book, Patrick Garry shows that despite the persistence of faith in bigger government and more regulation to help the 'little guy,' it is typically the rich that reap the benefits of big government. Anyone interested in understanding how big government really works needs to read this book."
   —**Todd J. Zywicki**, George Mason University Foundation
      Professor of Law at the Antonin Scalia Law School

"Garry makes a compelling case that bigger government not only fails to improve the life of ordinary Americans but actually harms them."
   —**Elizabeth Price Foley**, professor of law at Florida International University College of Law

"In this bold and brilliant book, Garry takes on our overgrown government in the terms of its defenders: he systematically demolishes the argument that a larger government better serves the poor and vulnerable. It is simply essential reading."
   —**Yuval Levin**, editor of *National Affairs*

"In this concise book, Garry uses concrete examples to show how and why big government inherently works against the very people it claims to help."
   —**Bradley A. Smith**, Josiah H. Blackmore II / Shirley M. Nault Professor of Law at Capital University Law School

the
FALSE PROMISE
of # BIG
GOVERNMENT

How Washington Helps
the Rich and Hurts the Poor

PATRICK M. GARRY

ISI
BOOKS

Wilmington, Delaware

Cataloging-in-Publication Data

Name: Garry, Patrick M.
Title: The false promise of big government : how Washington helps the rich and hurts the poor / by Patrick M Garry.
Description: Wilmington, Delaware : ISI Books, 2017.
Identifiers: LCCN 2017033874 | ISBN 9781610171441 (paperback)
Subjects: LCSH: United States—Social policy. | United States—Economic policy. | Federal government—United States. | Poor—Government policy—United States. | Working class—United States. | Middle class—United States. | BISAC: POLITICAL SCIENCE / Public Policy / Economic Policy. | BUSINESS & ECONOMICS / Public Finance.
Classification: LCC HN59.2 .G37 2017 | DDC 306.0973—dc23 LC record available at https://lccn.loc.gov/2017033874

Published in the United States by:

ISI Books
Intercollegiate Studies Institute
3901 Centerville Road
Wilmington, Delaware 19807-1938
www.isibooks.org

Manufactured in the United States of America

For Michael and Elizabeth

Contents

←——→

Introduction

←——→

EXPOSING THE MYTH
OF BIG GOVERNMENT

Since the New Deal, advocates for a stronger federal government have used poor, working-class, and middle-class Americans to justify their crusade. The argument asserts that government offers the only protection against the predations of the rich and powerful. It is as if government and the private economy represent mutually opposed constituencies: the economy serves the rich and powerful, and government represents the average person. So, to oppose a growing federal government is to oppose helping our most vulnerable citizens improve their lives.

This, anyway, has been the argument for the past eighty years.

Consider the generalized claim that the political system should ensure justice and opportunity for the average American. This argument makes the automatic assumption that the bigger government is, the more it helps the common person. And underlying this assumption is another assumption: that only bureaucratic agencies in Washington, D.C., can lift up the average person in all the ways that society apparently hobbles him or her.

By taking this position, advocates of big government cast their opponents as calloused enemies of the common person.

But many opponents of an ever-expanding government also contribute to the myth that they are uncaring. They do so by relying mainly on two arguments against big government: the cost argument and the constitutional argument. The first says that a huge federal apparatus creates wasteful government programs and imposes too great an economic burden on Americans. The second holds that the federal government—especially through the unelected administrative state—has broken through the limits on its authority that the U.S. Constitution put in place.

Both of these arguments are correct. Massive government programs are wasteful and impose huge economic costs on Americans, and many of them contradict constitutional provisions. But these arguments have not been sufficient to counter the claims of those clamoring for more and bigger government.

Ultimately, these arguments fall short because they do not go to the heart of the issue. They do not address the fact that the claims at the very core of the case for big government are simply false.

The truth is that big government often *hurts* the very people it purports to help—the poor, the working class, and the middle class. Actually, the problem is worse than that: big government frequently props up the rich, the powerful, and the politically connected.

This book does not focus on the arguments that limited-government proponents have traditionally used. Rather, it goes straight to the common-person justification for big government—a justification whose only legitimacy lies in the staying power of myth.

THE POLITICAL CAMPAIGN FOR BIG GOVERNMENT

From the Progressive era, through the New Deal and the Great Society, and right up to the present, many influential people have pushed for an expanded governmental role in all areas of social, cultural, and economic life. Calls for bigger government are now the predictable response to any social need or political issue. Big-government promises hold special appeal during times of emergency, when the public looks for an immediate savior. This emergency mentality led, for instance, to the passage of the Dodd-Frank Act in 2010—a law that substantially expanded, in ways that could not even be defined by the law, government regulation of the financial-services industry, from mega–Wall Street investment firms to small-town banks. Once the emergency passes, a more sober and rational public often reassesses the need for a bigger government—but by then, expanded government has been entrenched in law.

Recent experience bears out the constant growth of government. From 2000 to 2016, federal spending more than doubled, from $1.79 trillion to $3.85 trillion. Nearly 100,000 new federal rules have been issued since 1993, and the tax code is more than four million words long. According to the Competitive Enterprise Institute, federal agencies in 2016 issued 3,853 regulations, while Congress passed 214 new laws. That's 18 rules for every law enacted.

These numbers reflect a federal government that has broken free from constraints and that grows less and less accountable every year. As Charles Murray argues in his book *By the People: Rebuilding Liberty Without Permission*, the federal government is no longer an extension of the people through their elected representatives but an entity unto itself, beyond the effective control of the political process. In 1958 the National Election Study began asking the question "How much of the time do you trust the federal government to do what is right?" Seventy-three percent of respondents said "just about always" or "most of the time." Even as late as 1964, 77 percent of respondents so answered. But in a 2017 Pew Research Center poll, only 20 percent expressed such trust.

The reach of the federal government has become so extensive that it is nearly impossible to define any limits to its power. Laws such as the Dodd-Frank Act and the Affordable Care Act are so complicated that they cannot even be understood without a platoon of lawyers, and the complexity of the tax code masks all the ways it benefits special interests and hurts ordinary Americans.

Given the present size of government, perhaps the call should be for *defined government* rather than *limited government.* Decades of attacks by government expanders have cast those who call for limited government as being *anti*-government. Though a very small segment of the population may hold extreme anti-government attitudes, the opponents of unlimited government generally do not fit this stereotype. Instead they seek to protect the type of government structure outlined in the U.S. Constitution: a federal government strong in the roles and powers assigned to it, but limited to those roles and powers. Indeed, limited-government proponents value the integrity of government so much that they want to protect it from the inherent damage caused by overextension. As the federal government takes over functions previously performed by local governments or the private sector, it becomes overextended and breeds public distrust of its ability to address social problems competently.

Like anything good, government must be defined and contained. Few things are more pleasing and constructive than a fine meal, but everyone knows that there is a point when enjoyment turns to excess, when delight becomes disgust, when goodness yields to gluttony.

THE COMMON CASE AGAINST BIG GOVERNMENT

As noted, the case against ever-expanding government typically rests on two pillars: cost and constitutionality. Although these arguments do not refute the core claim of big-government proponents, they raise essential points that are worth reviewing:

The cost argument: As a share of the national economy, federal debt held by the public increased to more than 76 percent in 2016. This was the highest share since 1950. The figure was only 52 percent in President Barack Obama's first term. It is projected to rise to 85 percent in 2026.

The federal government's total debt approached $20 trillion at the end of 2016. In recent years, just its annual operating deficit has exceeded $1 trillion. These numbers are so immense as to be almost unfathomable.

As the government has grown, its focus has shifted from the provision of public goods to the facilitation of private consumption.

The entitlement state exemplifies the kind of debt-financed consumerist society big government has fostered. The unfunded liabilities of Social Security and Medicare alone amount to several times the national debt. And the rapid growth of the entitlement state contradicts even the advice of Franklin Delano Roosevelt, the president who introduced the modern welfare state. According to President Roosevelt: "The lessons of history . . . show conclusively that continued dependence upon relief induces a spiritual and moral disintegration fundamentally destructive to the national fiber. To dole out relief in this way is to administer a narcotic, a subtle destroyer of the human spirit." Roosevelt concluded, "The federal government must and shall quit this business of relief."

He said that in 1935.

From 1960 to 2010, the percentage of prospective workforce participants between the ages of eighteen and sixty-four receiving benefits from Social Security's disability insurance program rose almost tenfold, despite advances in medicine and life expectancy, not to mention the fact that a larger proportion of jobs did not involve hard labor.

Social-welfare policies since the 1960s have made it rational in the short term for people to behave in ways that would ensure poverty and dependency in the long term. And the more that people come to depend on government, the more they demand from government. This demand perpetuates and expands the entitlement system, which in turn fuels the growth of government.

The cost of government expansion can be seen in the sheer breadth of the Code of Federal Regulations, which now approaches two hundred thousand pages. Recent years have witnessed a marked increase in regulatory activity and burdens. The American Action Forum estimated that the regulations enacted during the Obama administration's first term cost $467 billion. The Dodd-Frank Act alone requires federal agencies to undertake almost four hundred different rule-making processes.

Aside from its cost, big government also has a negative effect on the overall economy. Government spending does not effectively stimulate private economic activity. In fact, government spending crowds out private spending and acts as a drag on the economy. Growth rates frequently decline when government spending consumes more than 25 percent of the economy.

The constitutional argument: Any study of the nation's founding documents, and particularly the *Federalist Papers*, reveals that although the framers meant to create a stronger federal government than had existed under the Articles of Confederation, they wanted the new federal government to be strong only in certain ways and areas. Much of the Constitution is dedicated to providing a structure of checks and balances to keep the federal government from exceeding its enumerated powers.

Despite these constitutional limits, the federal administrative state has grown dramatically over the past eight decades. This growth, across a wide array of areas, has followed a pattern. First, federal powers have expanded beyond their enumerated constitutional limits. Second, those powers have been delegated to agencies and away from elected representatives in Congress. Third, those agencies have been insulated from accountability. And finally, the courts have largely deferred to this delegation of power to government agencies.

According to Philip Hamburger in *Is Administrative Law Unlawful?*, the Constitution's checks and balances broke down in the early twentieth century. Progressives empowered government agencies, believing that "experts" would improve society much better than a government slowed by individual rights and a constitutionally mandated separation of powers. This progressive belief led to the New Deal, during which executive agencies came to act as an almost unchecked fourth branch of government. Professor Hamburger argues that the rise of the administrative state is essentially a reemergence of the arbitrary power that premodern monarchs asserted and that the U.S. Constitution was designed to prevent.

The usual response to criticisms like Hamburger's is that the complexities of modern life make the contemporary administrative state inevitable. But defenders of the modern administrative state do not address the dangers this bureaucratic apparatus poses to liberty and the integrity of self-government. Nor do they acknowledge that the administrative state undertakes destructive actions and is unresponsive to the constituencies on behalf of whom it claims to act.

Advocates of the administrative state argue that, because the legislative process can be slow, agencies should do more lawmaking. (Hence the 18:1 ratio of federal rules to laws.) Yet when the agency process itself slows down, advocates then argue that government is not sufficiently funded. But this ignores the fact that regulatory agency budgets have doubled and staffing has increased by more than 60 percent since the year 2000.

In 2009 the federal government set a post–World War II record for spending as a percentage of gross domestic product. The majority of budgets that President Obama submitted called for trillion-dollar deficits; no previous president had ever submitted a budget with such deficits. Obama's vision of government was reflected in an infographic advertisement his campaign released in 2012. "The Life of Julia" followed a fictional woman through every stage of her life, from shortly after birth to just after retirement, with each cartoon image celebrating her dependence on government.

The constitutional framers were wary of the kind of extensive federal government power displayed in "The Life of Julia." They did not view government as an evil, since the whole point of the Constitution was to create a stronger central government. But the framers did create a government that was limited in its scope. This is why they set up a system of checks and balances and separation of powers. And from a practical perspective, limits on government are essential because when government gets too big, it becomes ineffective and ill-equipped to handle basic governing functions.

THE FUNDAMENTAL ARGUMENT AGAINST BIG GOVERNMENT

This book will not reiterate the usual arguments against big government. It will not examine the cost of big government, nor the debt it imposes, nor the taxes it requires, nor the burdens it places on the economy. Nor will this book discuss the constitutional arguments against government—namely, the threat to liberty and the violation of the constitutional design of limited government through a system of checks and balances.

Rather, this book will address the very argument that is used to justify big government: that big government provides vital assistance to the average American. This argument is a myth. Instead of helping the average person at the expense of the wealthy, bigger government helps the politically powerful at the expense of the average person.

A strong and active federal government is necessary for various tasks, but when used as a panacea for society's problems, it often hurts those most in need of help. As government has grown so powerful in such far-reaching ways, it has become more aligned with the centers of power in society. It has fostered cronyism rather than competition. It has treated people more like passive clients than as active citizens. It has replaced opportunity with regulations that reinforce the status quo. It has favored government bureaucracy over individual well-being.

A well-functioning federal government is a cooperative actor in our civil society, working with local government and civic institutions to meet the diverse needs of a diverse society. Instead, our ever-expanding federal government has become a dictating force that has subdued the other actors and transformed a vibrant social fabric into a mass-manufactured, monochrome synthetic.

The goal of this book is to correct the myths underlying the explosive growth of modern government. The book does not seek to slash the federal government indiscriminately; it advocates for a federal government that is prudent, more focused, less susceptible to the corruptions of power, better run, more cooperative with all the other institutions of civil society, and more responsive to the real needs of the common person. Most important, no person or group should ever be sacrificed at the altar of government growth

This book lays out six key points about big government that are too rarely heard:

1. Big government caters to big power
2. Big government breeds cronyism
3. Big government is a tool of the elite
4. Big government becomes its own end
5. Big government backfires
6. Big government crowds out civil society

Good intentions aren't good enough. As author William Voegeli suggests in *The Pity Party*, big-government advocacy stems from a "strong preference for political stances that demonstrate one's heart is in the right place" and "a relative indifference to whether the policies based on those stances, as actually implemented, do or even can achieve their intended results."

But if we really want to help people, paying attention to results is essential. Too often, those who claim to speak for the "little guy" push for policies that don't help—and often harm—the most vulnerable in our society. This is the fundamental point that proponents of a defined government need to understand and communicate if they ever hope to curtail the seemingly endless growth of government.

Point #1

← →

BIG GOVERNMENT CATERS TO BIG POWER

Big government is all about monopoly. It exerts monopolistic power. It is justified by monopolistic power. It facilitates monopolistic power.

But this was not the American vision.

American history is rooted in opposition to monopolistic power. The early settlers came to America to escape the monopolistic authority of the established European religions. Much of the spirit for independence arose from the colonial opposition to chartered monopolies from England. The principle of freedom from monopolies became incorporated in various ways into the Constitution and was evident in early constitutional case law, such as

Trustees of Dartmouth College v. Woodward (1819) and *Charles River Bridge v. Warren Bridge* (1837).

The ideal of the independent yeoman farmer or artisan operating in an open and competitive marketplace dominated American self-identity through the nation's first century. Some states even banned monopolies in their state constitutions. Many other states, particularly midwestern and western states, ratified constitutional provisions combating the monopoly power of railroads and eastern banks. And the federal antitrust law, passed in the late nineteenth century, further expressed the American opposition to monopoly power.

Despite this long-standing national commitment to decentralized competition, the advocates of big government continue to push for a federal government that grows larger and less competitive day by day.

The New Deal era that spawned the big government of the modern age also witnessed the growth of industrial giants and the dominance of national media networks. Yet the nation has moved away from the large-scale, mass-industrialization model. Diversity, flexibility, and individualized choice now characterize American culture. A politics that kept up with these cultural changes would not attempt to concentrate ever more power in the federal government's vast administrative state but would disperse power in ways that made for more responsive, customized, and adaptive government.

Instead, the federal government gets bigger and more centralized. And as it does so, it drifts toward greater dysfunctionality. The top-down, one-size-fits-all approach is out of step with private society's use of dispersed knowledge and diverse consumer choices.

It is becoming more and more difficult for a centralized federal bureaucracy in Washington, D.C., to embody the diverse nation, and yet that is exactly what advocates of big government expect it to do. The federal government's centralized clumsiness became apparent in the Obama administration's 2016 man-

DID YOU KNOW?

In two decades, Fortune 100 companies grabbed a much larger share of the economy even as federal regulations grew by nearly 30 percent.

date that every public school in America comply with a federally initiated transgender restroom policy. The move overrode the authority of state and local school boards. At least thirteen states challenged the constitutionality of the directive in court.

All these problems are bad enough. But big government is damaging for still another reason: a strong correlation exists between the growth of government and the growth of other big centers of power.

BIG GOVERNMENT AND BIG BUSINESS

Proclaiming that they will fight for small businesses and defend the "little guy," advocates of big government insist that a powerful central government is needed to control the power of large, oligopolistic corporations.

But big government tends to entrench, not control,

big business. Big government, in fact, *prefers* big business. It is far easier to regulate an industry controlled by a few large corporations than one characterized by many small, competitive firms. And that's exactly the kinds of industries that are emerging. From 1994 to 2013, Fortune 100 companies increased their share of nominal GDP from 33 to 46 percent, while federal regulations grew nearly 30 percent. And by mid-2014, new business formation, measured as the share of all businesses less than a year old, had declined by roughly half since 1980.

Another prevailing myth holds that big business opposes big government. But just the reverse is true. Big corporations support big government. They are comfortable with increased regulation precisely because it hinders their competitors, making it harder for new businesses to form and for smaller firms to compete against bigger ones. Huge corporations can afford the costs of complying with regulations, but those same costs can drive smaller or newer companies out of business. Furthermore, the biggest businesses can afford expensive lobbyists to manipulate government bureaucracies to act in their interests. And the more corporate welfare that big government doles out to big business, the more allegiance and complicity that big government acquires from big business.

The effects of government's widening regulatory umbrella are especially evident in the financial services arena. The CEO of Goldman Sachs, Lloyd Blankfein, acknowledged that his company was a big beneficiary of the Dodd-Frank Act's complex regulatory requirements, which have "raised the barriers to entry into the banking business higher than at any other time in modern history." JPMorgan Chase's CEO, Jamie Dimon, said the same thing, explaining that Dodd-Frank helped create a "bigger moat" that protected the huge banks from competition. Sure enough, the big investment banks and brokerage firms have seen record profits since the Dodd-Frank Act was passed.

According to the Federal Deposit Insurance Corporation, thousands of commercial banks have disappeared since Dodd-Frank. Between 2010 and 2015, only two new banks were chartered. By comparison, in the quarter century prior to 2008, an average of one hundred new banks were chartered each year. Even during the Great Depression of the 1930s, an average of nineteen new banks a year were chartered.

Big government's favoritism toward big business and big money can be seen in the way the government tried to stimulate the economy in the wake of the 2008 recession. The federal government increased its taxes and regulation of the economy, thereby inhibiting job hiring through business growth and new business start-ups. Meanwhile, following a monetary program known as "quantitative easing," the Federal Reserve bought trillions of dollars of the federal government's debt in the form of bonds. This program did not create new jobs or increase the incomes of lower- and middle-class America; instead, it boosted the profits of Wall Street bond brokers and wealthy investors who owned equities in the stock market.

In short, big government and big business exist in a kind of alliance, each feeding off the other. Through regulation, government preserves big business by driving off smaller competitors; by protecting big business, politicians buy allegiance and ensure the continual flow of campaign contributions from corporations.

HOW BIG GOVERNMENT HURTS THE SMALL AND POWERLESS

The government's corporate welfare fosters bigger and more monopolistic corporations while hurting smaller competitors. The effects of the Dodd-Frank Act on the financial services industry offer just one example of how this works. Consider, too, the rollout of the Affordable Care Act (ACA), which transferred massive authority from individuals and employers to the federal bureaucracy.

The ACA's regulatory scheme helped the big players in the health-care field and hurt the small ones. An August 2, 2012, headline in the *Wall Street Journal* announced, "Small Firms See Pain in Health Law." The article pointed out that ACA compliance costs burdened small businesses to a much larger degree than big businesses, and thereby spurred industry consolidation. Solo physicians and small groups, for instance, could not afford to purchase and maintain the electronic records needed to comply with government reporting requirements. From 2008 to 2014, the number of independent physicians declined by almost 50 percent. Large hospitals bought up smaller physician practices and outpatient service providers to form big health-care networks. In 2015, 112 hospital mergers occurred, an increase of 18 percent from the previous year. As the *Wall Street Journal* noted in an article dated September 22, 2015, this ACA-fueled health-care "merger frenzy" transformed the medical marketplace into "a land of giants."

The goal of the ACA was to promote choice and competition. But it produced the opposite. From 2013 to 2017, the number of insurers selling plans in the individual markets dropped 45 percent, from 395 to 218. As of late 2016, one-third of all U.S. counties had only one health insurer offering coverage on the ACA marketplace. Citing the federal government's own data, *Business Insider* reported that twenty-five of the thirty-eight states with individual insurance exchanges run through the federal HealthCare.gov platform saw the number of available insurers decrease in 2017.

By actively supporting politically favored corporations, and by pushing industry consolidation in ways that drive out smaller competitors, the ACA demonstrated once again big government's preference for dealing with monopolistic markets dominated by large corporate players.

The architects of the ACA deliberately sought consolidation in the health-care industry. They argued, wrongly, that size would lead to better care and more efficiency. But size would also make medical care easier to regulate from Washington, D.C.

Through the ACA, the Dodd-Frank Act, and many other efforts, the federal government creates incentives for businesses to get inefficiently large. And then once they get so large, the government has more justification for regulating, since they are so large that they may be "too big to fail."

Thus, big government and big business have an implicit quid pro quo arrangement. The bigger the corporations, the easier it is for government to regulate them. And the bigger the government, the more protection that big business has against smaller competitors.

BIG GOVERNMENT'S DENIAL OF OPPORTUNITIES

Traditional public education exemplifies the way in which government favors monopolies in society, to the detriment of the common person.

Education is the most valuable tool for escaping poverty and achieving upward mobility. But the federal government ignores the connection between economic mobility and education when it creates public-sector monopolies in primary and secondary education. Education is treated like just another social-welfare program, with continual increases in public spending that serve primarily to expand the government bureaucracy. It is treated like a public utility—a state-sponsored monopoly that offers a standardized product indifferent to individual needs and administered by a vast bureaucracy.

Consequently, the American educational system is failing many young people. In particular, it is failing the young people who need it most—the poor and disadvantaged.

At the primary and secondary level, government education spending has soared in recent decades. Per-pupil federal education spending is nearly four times its 1970 level. Public schools all across the nation have added staff at a much more rapid pace than student enrollment has increased. The District of Columbia public schools, for instance, increased their staffing by 7.7 percent from 1993 to 2014 even as enrollment *declined* by 3.1 percent.

Despite the increases in spending and staffing, student performance has not improved. According to the Nation's Report Card, only 25 percent of all twelfth graders were proficient in math in 2015, with just 7 percent of black students being proficient. In a February 2015 report, the Educational Testing Service reported that American millennials lag behind their peers in other countries in literacy, numeracy, and problem solving. Youth from poor and minority households drop out of school at alarming rates, and many of those who do graduate from public high schools do not have the skills to continue their education or acquire a job with any meaningful future prospects.

Yet government continues to try to maintain its monopoly. It does everything it can to prevent competition in the education field. Public-sector educators staunchly resist programs that would give all students, regardless of family income, the chance to attend the school of their choice.

As it now stands, the wealthy can attend any school they choose, but the poor and working class are stuck with the public schools assigned to them, regardless of the quality of those schools. Furthermore, the morass of government regulations stymies local charter and private schools seeking to reach out to poor and middle-class communities. Accreditation mandates and limits on the number of charter schools all reduce the supply of alternative schools.

Policies like charter schooling, vouchers, and school choice have succeeded whenever they have been implemented, especially in benefiting needy children. The data consistently show that voucher recipients or school-choice students academically outperform their counterparts from traditional public schools. In a 2007 study, scholars from Harvard and the Brookings Institution found that school vouchers in New York City significantly increased the proportion of African American students who went on to college. A 2009 study out of Stanford University shows that access to charter schools reduced New York City's black-white achievement gap by 66 percent in reading and 86 percent in math.

Eighty percent of the charter schools in New York City outperform their comparable public schools. The 6,700 students at New York's twenty-two Success Academy charter schools, overwhelmingly from poor, minority families, scored in the top 1 percent in math and top 7 percent in English on recent state tests. Some 90 percent of the students at Success Academy's Central Harlem charter schools scored proficient on the state's math exams in 2015; just 15 percent of students in Central Harlem's traditional public schools scored proficient.

The issue is not funding. Charter schools on average spend significantly less than traditional public schools. For example, in her book *The Prize: Who's in Charge of America's Schools?*, veteran reporter Dale Russakoff notes that charter schools in Newark, New Jersey, spent $16,400 per pupil in 2014–15, whereas Newark's district schools spent $19,650—17 percent more.

One big difference is in *how* charter schools spend their money. Russakoff's data show that less than half of the traditional public school's spending ($9,604 per pupil) trickled down to the classroom. By contrast, three-quarters of the charter school money ($12,664 per pupil) went into the classroom. *New York Times* columnist Joe Nocera put it well when he wrote: "Money that the charter school is spending on extra support [for students] is being soaked up by the bloated bureaucracy in the public school system. It is a devastating fact."

Despite this performance record, federal and state governments continue to oppose voucher programs, primarily because they might upset the status quo, protected by powerful public-employee unions. In 2013 the U.S. Justice Department sued to block Louisiana's voucher program on the grounds that it violated forty-year-old federal desegregation orders, even though 90 percent of the beneficiaries of the scholarships awarded under the Louisiana program were African American. And New York City mayor Bill de Blasio blocked a Success Academy middle school in Harlem from adding 194 students, all of whom were low-income minority students attending a Success Academy elementary school, even though on state assessment tests 80 percent of those students passed the math test and 59 percent passed the English test. Meanwhile, at the public middle school that most of the students would be forced to attend instead, just 5 percent of students passed the math test and 11 percent the English test.

"THE GOVERNMENT IS SO VAST"

President Obama told Congress in September 2009 that the health-care reform law would not add "one dime to our deficits, either now or in the future." All the increased benefits being promised under the ACA would be paid for out of cost savings from a reform of a Medicare and Medicaid system that was "full of abuse and waste." In other words, the ACA would extend health insurance to thirty million uninsured Americans while improving health care for millions more already-insured Americans and yet not increase the deficit at all, just because Medicare and Medicaid would finally get cleaned up.

What a cleaning up that would be!

But this argument itself undermines the case for big government. If Medicare and Medicaid, which accounted for nearly 20 percent of all federal spending in 2009, were that full of waste and inefficiency, why were the programs not reformed earlier? And if two government programs became so full of waste that their reform could pay for the biggest government social program since the Great Society era, does that not say something about how unaccountable big-government programs inevitably become?

And if such waste cannot be eliminated after almost a half century, then how can big government ever be held accountable? Today there is one member of Congress for every 5,150 civilian members of the executive branch. How can our elected representatives possibly keep track of the activities of all those bureaucrats, let alone control their actions and prevent "abuse and waste"?

Government has grown far too big, as an unexpected source acknowledged in 2013. When it emerged that the Internal Revenue Service (IRS) had committed blatant abuses by targeting conservative groups, longtime Obama adviser David Axelrod defended the president's ignorance of the scandal by saying, "Part of being president is that there is so much beneath you that you can't know because the government is so vast."

This statement constitutes perhaps the strongest argument that government has become too big. Even an administration that actively expanded the federal government to its largest size in U.S. history admitted that it was too vast for the president to know what is going on with it.

But the government expanders don't acknowledge these points. To them, big government is never big enough.

Point #2

←——→

BIG GOVERNMENT BREEDS CRONYISM

By definition, government is controlled by politics. So as government grows in size and influence, political connections increasingly determine social and economic relations.

The rising prominence of politics benefits the politically connected and marginalizes the common person, for whom champions of big government claim to stand.

The advocates of big government often make a big issue of limiting the influence of the wealthy and the politically powerful. Their favored approach is usually campaign finance reform, or "getting big money out of politics," as many progressives put it. But their concerns about how much wealthy individuals and corporations give to political campaigns only underscore the reality that big government and the politically powerful work hand in hand.

If they really wanted to limit the political (and therefore social and economic) influence of "big money," the best reform would be to reduce the size and scope of government.

Government will always respond to political pressures, and the stronger the faction, the stronger the pressure. This is one of the reasons the framers favored limited government: to restrict the influence of political factions.

The case of General Electric (GE) illustrates how the powerful can partner with big government. In 2015 the Capital Research Center reported that GE had spent more than $300 million on lobbying since 1998. Its CEO visited the White House dozens of times. The progressive group Americans for Tax Fairness states that GE paid no federal income taxes from 2008 to 2012 and received $3.1 billion in refunds, despite earning $27.5 billion in profits during the same period. Even if this estimate is exaggerated, GE paid nowhere near the statutory rate of 35 percent in income taxes.

General Electric also reaped benefits from the Obama administration's "green economy" spending. GE received more than $2 billion in federal loan guarantees for wind and solar projects. Moreover, it invested heavily in a company that made lithium-ion batteries for electric cars; that company received $132 million in federal stimulus funds—and then went bankrupt. All these government benefits occurred because GE has the resources to lobby federal officials and work the corporate tax code to its benefit, while smaller rivals do not.

There is a term for government's favoritism toward the politically connected: *crony capitalism.*

Crony capitalism is everywhere. Almost every major corporation and trade group has set up lobbying offices in Washington, D.C. This is no accident. Countless studies have shown a massive return on investment from lobbying. And as government grows, lobbying only becomes more important. Companies used to try, as Ronald Reagan once put it, to get government off their backs. But in the age of cronyism, the goal of lobbying has changed. Now corporations try to convince government to grant them special privileges and subsidies. And just as big business can more easily shoulder high regulatory costs, it is also the best positioned to lobby for special benefits from an ever-expanding government.

The tax code exemplifies how big government inevitably favors the more powerful. Higher tax rates, needed to finance bigger government, are almost always accompanied by loopholes that the wealthy and their lobbyists are most able to exploit. Consider the tax increases Illinois implemented under former governor Pat Quinn. A $2 billion tax increase, the largest in Illinois history, was the state legislature's remedy for a severe budget deficit. But as soon as the tax increase went into effect for all Illinois businesses, the largest and most influential corporations started cashing in their special tax breaks. The small and medium-sized businesses that could not afford lobbyists were stuck paying the higher tax rates. So the 1 percent of politically connected businesses prospered at the expense of the 99 percent.

Cronyism can exist even when government on the surface takes an adversarial approach to particular parties or industries. For instance, even though the Dodd-Frank Act imposed significant regulations on Wall Street, the government simultaneously gave Wall Street very favorable treatment. After the 2008 financial crisis, big banks paid fines rather than face prosecution. Some 839 people had been convicted for their roles in the savings and loan scandals of the 1980s; only one Wall Street executive was convicted as a result of the 2008 financial crisis.

Government cronyism can also be seen in the controversial Supreme Court decision in *Kelo v. City of New London* (2005). In that case, the court said that the city of New London, Connecticut, had the right to seize, in a process known as eminent domain, the homes of private individuals and transfer them to a different private owner for the purposes of economic development. So poor and working-class people lost their homes, and the city government handed the land over to a politically influential entity: the nonprofit New London Development Corporation (NLDC). The NLDC's major client for the proposed redevelopment was the Pfizer Corporation, then the largest pharmaceutical producer in the world.

In *The Grasping Hand: "Kelo v. City of New London" and the Limits of Eminent Domain*, legal scholar Ilya

Somin reports that *Kelo* did what government property takings for private redevelopment so often do: it lined the pockets of developers and the politically connected while disproportionately burdening the poor and minorities. Because the New London neighborhood had seen better days, government and its private developers apparently felt justified in taking working-class homes to make way for the kinds of neighborhoods favored by high-income urban professionals.

The proposed economic development never did get built, despite a $78 million incentive package from the state of Connecticut. And just four years after the Supreme Court decision, Pfizer abandoned its New London facilities.

But the people whose properties the government seized were still out of their homes.

CRONYISM ALWAYS FINDS INROADS

When government grows, so does crony capitalism. Here again, the Dodd-Frank Act and the Affordable Care Act (ACA), two of the biggest federal ventures in recent history, illustrate the point well.

Dodd-Frank gives special protection to the "too big to fail" financial institutions. Those institutions now receive favorable treatment from creditors, who see that the federal government protects the big banks. The law thus protects the *lenders* to big banks against loss as well, allowing the largest and most influential banks to attract investment capital at a much lower cost. Moreover, as

Dodd-Frank regulations have forced community banks to withdraw from the mortgage business, bigger banks have acquired even greater market share and are using this monopoly power to extract higher profits.

The ACA favored the big insurance companies by forcing individuals to buy their product. To persuade insurance companies to play along with the law, the ACA also promised to subsidize insurer losses from policies sold on the law's exchanges. Insurers agreed not to price their insurance products in ways that rationally took account of the distorted risk profiles the law required; to make up for this irrational and unsustainable pricing practice, the government cushioned their losses with taxpayer dollars.

Under the ACA, health insurers virtually became clients of the federal government. The big insurance companies could take more risk and cut their premiums to gain market share, knowing that the taxpayers would cover their losses. In 2016 alone the federal government subsidized exchange insurers to the tune of $32.8 billion, according to the Center for Health and Economy. Considering how vehemently ACA supporters attacked the greed of insurance companies, it is surprising that the law made the government responsible for insurers' bottom lines. And insurance subsidies were just the beginning; the ACA initiated government payouts to a wide array of business and trade groups with a stake in American health care.

The ACA's cronyism was also evident in the various waivers the federal government gave to preferred groups. As early as 2013, the government had already issued waivers to unions representing more than half a million workers. By contrast, the Obama administration had issued waivers for fewer than seventy thousand nonunion workers. Likewise, big business received a waiver from the employer mandate—while the mandate for individuals to purchase insurance remained unchanged.

HYPOCRISY

Cronyism breeds hypocrisy. On the campaign trail and in media appearances, politicians who advocate for big government often denounce big business. But in practice, they reward and strengthen big business—or at least favored businesses.

In 2015, big-government advocates fiercely defended the Export-Import Bank, despite their strong campaign rhetoric against corporate welfare. The Export-Import Bank, a federal agency that effectively delivers corporate welfare to very large businesses, helps selected American exporters compete in overseas markets by providing tax-payer-backed loan guarantees to foreign customers. The bank's benefits flow overwhelmingly to giant U.S. corporations that spend millions of dollars on lobbying. In 2013, 30 percent of the subsidies went to Boeing, with General Electric receiving 10 percent, Bechtel 7 percent, and Caterpillar 5 percent. The bank dedicates twice as much financing just to the sales of Boeing aircraft as it does to the exports of every small business in America combined.

In the congressional debate over reauthorization of the Export-Import Bank, in 2012, the most vocal opponents of big business pushed hardest for reauthorization. Their desire for bigger government seemed to overwhelm any opposition to corporate welfare. As a presidential candidate in 2008, Barack Obama had denounced the Export-Import Bank as "little more than a fund for corporate welfare." But as president, Obama signed the reauthorization bill into law, touting the bank's great economic value.

Many of those who speak out against special privileges for big business nonetheless want to maintain big government's close relationship with big business—by making big business more dependent on big government.

> ## THOUGHTS ON BIG GOVERNMENT
>
> "If the U.S. is going to tackle its many problems, we are going to have to find ways to encourage would-be entrepreneurs to start innovative, productive businesses, rather than dedicating their efforts to co-opting government in order to secure economic advantage."
>
> —Robert E. Litan and Ian Hathaway, *Harvard Business Review*

THE RISE OF INTEREST GROUPS

President Lyndon Johnson once said that the political fate of big government would be determined by how many benefits it could deliver. Knowing that big government has to provide big benefits in order to survive, interest groups form to petition government for those benefits. Big government and big interest groups then become interlocked as they both grow in power and feed off each other.

Big government thus breeds big interest groups and ends up focusing more on empowering those interest groups than on empowering individuals. The public becomes merely an indirect client of government, in a condition the political scientist Theodore Lowi once called interest-group liberalism. When interest groups become government's primary constituents, public governance becomes a closed process of negotiation between career bureaucrats and the executive officers of interest groups, who determine how government benefits get doled out. Interest groups push for bigger government so as to get bigger benefits. At the same time, the government supports bigger interest groups, since interest groups are easier to manage than are diverse individuals.

Interest-group liberalism frequently leads government to limit the growth of new businesses and new ways of doing business. Although innovative approaches can provide much improved products or services as well as new work opportunities, government regulators try to lock in old arrangements that established interest groups want to maintain. Consider the way government has treated the transportation service Uber. Especially in its early years, Uber struggled to get government clearance to operate in many jurisdictions. Despite its incredible popularity and customized service, government's web of regulations kept Uber out—not least because the old taxi companies and unions wanted it that way.

Interest-group government exacerbates the inequality that champions of big government claim to combat. Overregulation stymies the kinds of service industries that have historically offered opportunities to poorer individuals. Think of barbershops, transportation businesses, and street vending, all of which are heavily regulated. Conversely, anyone is free to start an app business. No government officials check credentials or certifications in the tech sector. Meanwhile, a hair braider needs to earn a degree, pass tests, and take continuing education courses to braid hair. This inequality further burdens Americans with fewer educational opportunities and jeopardizes their ability to work. Nearly one in three occupations in this country now requires some kind of licensing permission from the government.

THE INSTITUTIONAL CORRUPTION OF BIG GOVERNMENT

In *A Republic No More: Big Government and the Rise of American Political Corruption*, Jay Cost argues that the growth of government corrupts our republican system of government and sacrifices the public interest for the benefit of a privileged few.

This is institutional corruption, not individual corruption. It does not rely on public officials' taking bribes or otherwise acting in intentionally corrupt ways. Instead, institutional corruption occurs because the institutions of government that the framers designed in the eighteenth century are incapable of handling all the additional powers that government has taken on over the past two centuries. In other words, the expansion of government power has broken down the system of checks and balances. With its essential institutions overloaded, government behaves irresponsibly, which leads to corruption.

As Cost shows, New Deal programs that began with good intentions ended up being instruments of political corruption. President Roosevelt probably never thought the National Industrial Recovery Act would end up mired in corruption and hurting those it was meant to help, such as labor and consumers—but that is precisely what happened. And such corruption developed because government had taken on far more power than its institutions could constrain.

Decades have elapsed since the New Deal made big government a fixture of American life. The problems of institutional corruption and cronyism haven't gone away. And they never will unless we address the fundamental issue: big government itself.

Point #3

←——→

BIG GOVERNMENT IS A TOOL OF THE ELITE

The most consistent trait of modern liberalism is its belief in continually expanding the scope and power of government.

This is a drastic reversal from its historical stance.

Classical liberalism, as it existed during the eighteenth and nineteenth centuries, believed that limited government provided the most important protection for liberty. The shift toward bigger government began with the rise of progressivism in the late nineteenth century.

During the early twentieth century, progressivism was essentially a reform group within the Republican Party, with President Theodore Roosevelt as its leader.

Progressives championed, for instance, civil service reform, new regulations regarding food and drug safety, and child labor reform. These policies required a more active federal government, but one devoted to promoting market competition and middle-class mobility.

When Roosevelt left the presidency, however, the progressive movement departed from its Republican Party foundations. The later brand of progressivism looked to transform the country radically through a much-expanded federal government.

Progressivism believed strongly in a government of experts. To facilitate and exercise this expertise, administrative agencies would proliferate and grow more powerful. And the more numerous and powerful the agencies, the bigger and more powerful the federal government.

Progressivism contradicted the Constitution's profound skepticism toward unchecked power. The Constitution was not intended to be a blueprint for rule by an elite group of experts; rather, its system of checks and balances was designed to prevent a small group from exercising unlimited or arbitrary power. The framers believed that the most democratic and sustainable system of government would enable the public to administer control, even if this control meant that the government sometimes acted slowly and inefficiently.

Progressivism's confidence in government run by experts reflected a paternalistic sense that elites could make the best decisions for the less educated or enlightened common person. The elitist paternalism of progressives can be seen in their historical association with eugenics. Progressives supported compulsory sterilization of people deemed mentally ill or otherwise deficient. This policy violated fundamental individual liberties and resulted in the forced sterilization of many healthy and normal, albeit poor, citizens.

Fortunately, eugenics no longer features prominently in mainstream progressive thought. But elitism and paternalism—the notion that "experts" know best how to help the common person—remain central to big-government progressivism.

> **DID YOU KNOW?**
>
> By the end of 2016, America's four richest counties were all suburbs of Washington, D.C. The explosive growth of government is good for the political class.

THE RISE OF THE POLITICAL CLASS

The progressive faith in a much-expanded, expert-run federal government inspired the New Deal and animates modern-day liberalism. Through the influence of modern progressivism, the executive branch and its agencies have become the primary governing entity of society. This trend has frozen out the common person from a more meaningful democratic role in society.

Elites often use the poor to justify government expansion. They claim that only government can help the poor and then argue that government must be so much larger so as to fulfill these needs. But in the end, the poor are still poor—only this time, they are dependent on a larger government. The only people who benefit are the progressive elite, who by controlling government gain more control over society.

The progressive drive for an ever-expanding government has led to an ever-expanding professional bureaucracy to manage that government. This bureaucracy in turn devotes itself to further expanding government and to cementing its control over that government. Thus, a mutually reinforcing circle occurs—the formation of a political class, which then contributes to bigger government, which then requires a larger political class, and so on and so forth. The bigger that government becomes, the more distant it is from the public, and the more an elite political class controls it.

One indication that big government has spawned an elite political class can be found in how the nation's capital has prospered. While the rest of the country struggled to recover from the 2008 recession, Washington, D.C., thrived as the federal government dramatically expanded. By 2012, the Washington metropolitan region claimed seven of the nation's ten wealthiest counties. A June 1, 2013, *Wall Street Journal* headline stated, "Washington Booms as a New Gilded Age Takes Root." At the end of 2016, the Census Bureau reported that America's four richest counties were all suburbs of D.C.

Big government, as controlled by the political elite, is inherently prone to lose its connection to the public interest. As the eminent philosopher Reinhold Niebuhr wrote, big centralized governments are inevitably immoral, since people are capable of moral good only in small communities. According to Niebuhr, human beings are too self-serving and limited in imagination to treat people outside their sphere of personal contacts with the kind of care and respect those people deserve.

Moreover, the elite often have interests diametrically opposed to those of the average person. For instance, reducing the levels of unskilled, low-wage immigration, while beneficial to the working class, would be detrimental to elites in cities like Los Angeles and New York. Luxury and tourism businesses dependent on low-wage, unskilled foreign-born labor would face much higher costs if that labor source was restricted.

A recent example of the public's antagonism to elite rule can be found in Britain's 2016 vote to exit the European Union (EU). Polls showed that a majority of British citizens opposed the broad transfer of power from a democratic nation-state to an undemocratic supranational institution. For instance, every EU nation member had to submit its budget for approval to the European Commission, an unelected supranational bureaucracy, before that budget could even be submitted to the nation's own parliament. The Brexit vote, then, demonstrated that, in the opinion of the British public, the EU had become increasingly unrepresentative of and unaccountable to the democratic will of British citizens.

The EU elites were quick to call Brexit supporters racist, intolerant, and reactionary. This was the EU's means of avoiding the real argument against it—namely, that it had become an undemocratic institution unresponsive to the general public.

The virulent attacks on Brexit supporters also ignored the EU's obvious failures. After seventeen years of the euro, the economies of France, Spain, Italy, Portugal, and Greece remained in long-term stagnation. Youth unemployment rates in Spain and Italy had reached 45 percent and 37 percent, respectively, and Greece was in a state of economic collapse. But perhaps the EU's greatest failing lay in the fact that its decades of regulations had not brought the nations of the continent any closer together.

The issues raised by Brexit parallel those emerging with American federalism. The rise of the Tea Party and then of the Donald Trump presidential campaign can be directly attributed to the increasing centralization and arrogance of the federal government. The public has become frustrated with a federal government run largely by an unelected cadre of experts that reaches further into everyday life with each passing year. The average person wishes to control his or her own destiny through local communities, but elites favor putting power in the hands of an increasingly distant and single-minded group of people who see themselves as society's anointed leaders.

The United States, for most of its history fertile ground for local self-government, has witnessed almost as much cosmopolitan centralization as has Europe. And similar to social movements in Europe, Americans have rebelled against elites, who often escape the consequences of their failures.

The public has become disillusioned by a federal government controlled by highly credentialed people who nonetheless took the nation to near economic collapse in 2008, who have put the country $20 trillion in debt, and whose antipoverty programs have failed to eliminate poverty and have only built up government bureaucracies.

THE STATUS CULTURE OF BIG GOVERNMENT

Centralization also hurts the poor and working class because big government tends to perpetuate a status culture rather than building a growth culture that empowers upward mobility for the common person. Big government distributes benefits to individuals based on their particular economic status; legal protections are conferred depending on one's particular social or demographic status.

A focus on status is not all bad. For instance, government safety nets can be valuable, focusing on the status of an individual when that individual slips into a condition of poverty. Safety nets can catch those people who find themselves hit by economic crises and prevent them from living lives of abject poverty.

The problem is that too much of a focus on status can become confining. Security is a valuable but limited goal. Growth and mobility are needed to propel people out of poverty and into a more prosperous state of life.

A danger of many big-government social-welfare programs is that they can make people permanently dependent on a program that was meant to be temporary. Government programs often just sustain low-income people in their current status rather than providing them a springboard to the middle class. As polls continually show, poor and working-class Americans do not strive for a life of subsistence. They seek a culture of growth, not a culture of status. It is the wealthy who are interested in protecting social and economic status—their own.

As an indication of people's desire for growth cultures, the evidence shows that high-tax, high-spending, and highly regulated states suffer high rates of out-migration. People are leaving these states because opportunities are drying up. Indeed, high-tax, high-spending, and highly regulated states increasingly house only the very rich and the very poor, along with the millions of government workers who belong to powerful public-employee unions.

Government can suppress the growth energy of the private sector by creating economic ceilings. Occupational licensing, for instance, hits low-income people especially hard. Such licensing requirements may make sense for surgeons and architects, but not for a lot of other jobs that could provide a path out of poverty. Jobs like hairdresser, teeth whitener, and real estate salesperson are among those most protected by licensing restrictions. Although these regulations do little to improve quality or safety, they make it difficult for people with limited time and resources to improve their lives by acquiring a new trade.

Licenses for low- and middle-income professions on average cost more than $200 and require nine months of training, according to the Institute for Justice. It takes 372 days on average to become a licensed cosmetologist, but only 33 days to become an emergency medical technician. In several states, a hair-braiding license requires 1,500 hours of training and multiple exams. In the District of Columbia, a shoe shiner must get four different licenses at a cost of more than $300.

In the 1950s, fewer than 5 percent of jobs required licenses. By 2008, almost 30 percent required licenses.

These licensing requirements hurt consumers as well, because businesses pass on the costs of compliance to the customers. For example, the restrictive requirements to become a nurse practitioner have been found to increase the price of a child's medical exam by as much as 16 percent.

The morass of big-government regulation chokes economic growth. Approximately 350,000 more federal regulations existed in 2016 than in 1989. The cost of this regulatory web amounted to more than $2 trillion each year. The Obama administration added some 20,642 new regulations in 2015 alone, at a cost of more than $22 billion annually. The Mercatus Center estimated that government regulation had caused a 25 percent reduction in the U.S. economy from 1980 to 2012, meaning that the economy was about $4 trillion smaller in 2012 than it would have been had 1980 regulatory levels held steady. This amounted to a loss in real income of approximately $13,000 for every American. The Mercatus Center also found that federal regulations are about six to eight times more costly for low-income households than for high-income ones. And the higher the regulatory cost, the more difficult and costly it is for low- and middle-class entrepreneurs to start a business.

THE ECONOMIC DISTORTIONS OF BIG GOVERNMENT

Big-government advocates claim that increased government involvement in the economy is needed to give lower-income people a chance at economic advancement.

But time and again government spending has failed in this regard.

The $831 billion federal stimulus program passed in 2009, which exceeded all previous U.S. economic

THOUGHTS ON BIG GOVERNMENT

"While some [government] policy initiatives support small business, others directly harm them, but many others confound small-business owners by creating a complicated, ever changing matrix of regulations, programs, incentives, and deterrents that make business decisions more difficult and time consuming."

—National Federation of Independent Business Research Foundation, *Small Business Problems and Priorities*

stimulus programs combined, had a negligible effect on the economy and the incomes of average Americans. In addition to that stimulus package, the Federal Reserve injected another $3 trillion into the banking system in an effort to boost the economy. Despite all this spending, not once in the subsequent seven years did the economy even get close to the average rate of growth that prevailed from 1948 to 2007.

The lesson here is that government spending, especially when accompanied by increased regulation, cannot produce the kind of growth and opportunity that the private sector can. A vibrant and energetic private sector best promotes a culture of transformational growth and upward mobility. But as the public sector expands, the private sector shrinks. The Obama recovery was the weakest recovery since the Great Depression, in large part because the flood of government spending drowned out the more productive, job-creating private investing.

Big-government advocates dismiss growth, as if it were something only the rich want. But the lowest-income classes need growth far more than do the rich, who already have their wealth.

During the escalating government involvement following the 2008 recession, the Americans most in need of economic advancement suffered the most. Government spending increased so much that the federal debt held by the public, as a share of GDP, grew from approximately 30 percent in 2001 to nearly 80 percent in 2014—and yet median household incomes declined. Households headed by single women saw their incomes fall by roughly 7 percent. People under the age of twenty-five experienced a decline of almost 10 percent. Black heads of households had their income fall by almost 11 percent. The incomes of workers with a high school diploma or less fell by approximately 8 percent. This is all a dramatic reversal of the progress these groups experienced during the expansions of the 1980s and 1990s.

The number of people receiving food stamps reached an all-time high in 2013. Seven million more people were living in poverty in 2015 than in 2009. And the black poverty rate reached more than 26 percent in 2014.

In an attempt to stimulate the economy artificially, the Federal Reserve embarked on its quantitative easing (QE) program, an unprecedented purchase of government bonds on the open market to keep interest rates near zero. Not only did this bond-buying program fail to produce vibrant economic growth, but it also hurt many average Americans, particularly senior citizens. Because interest rates went to near zero, and because senior citizens depend on interest from savings to fund their retirement, households headed by seniors seventy-five and older lost on average $2,700 in annual income.

The Federal Reserve's QE program was the largest financial-markets intervention by any government in history. Economic experts estimate that the trillions spent by the Fed yielded a minuscule total return of 0.25 percent of GDP. But the program was a bonanza for Wall Street, leading to a surging stock market that substantially increased the wealth of the richest Americans, who had significant stock investments. The QE program also benefited the big banks, which enjoyed lowered loan costs, huge gains on the values of their securities holdings, and fat commissions from brokering most of the Fed's QE transactions.

In the wake of the 2008 recession, Wall Street had its most profitable years ever. But the Fed policy did nothing to combat wage stagnation or the reduced share of wages in the national income.

The QE program shows how the federal government's increased size and power has concentrated wealth in fewer hands. QE was intended to counteract growth-suppressing fiscal policies (higher government spending, taxes, and regulatory activity), but in the end the rich got richer at the expense of savers and average people.

BIG GOVERNMENT CAN UNDERMINE MOBILITY

If there is one factor that has energized and guided America, it is the middle class. But big government is contributing to a shrinking middle class.

Middle-class incomes and opportunities for mobility have declined, despite a robust stock market that has greatly enriched the wealthy. A polarization or hollowing out of the labor market has eliminated many of the jobs traditionally available to the middle class. The wealthy and highly educated are doing well, and the number of low-wage, unskilled jobs are increasing, as are government benefits to low-income individuals. But the middle class is struggling.

Government policies are growing the gap between the elite and the middle class. Working-class employees have seen their payroll deductions increase during the past decade, while private-equity partners who make millions have enjoyed much more favorable tax treatment. The carried-interest exemption allows hedge-fund managers to treat their incomes as capital gains, taxed at a significantly lower rate than are wages. Nor do Social Security and Medicare taxes apply to capital-gains distributions received by these Wall Street investors.

According to the Pew Research Center, 61 percent of all adults lived in middle-income households in the early 1970s. By 2012, that figure had fallen to 51 percent. Meanwhile, the percentages living in upper- and lower-income households both increased. The middle-class share of national income fell from 62 percent in 1989 to 45 percent in 2012, while the share of national income received by upper-income households rose from 29 percent to 46 percent. From 2009 to 2014, the percentage of Americans who considered themselves "middle class" fell from 53 to 44 percent. Correspondingly, the median household income in the United States fell by more than $1,000.

The political elites who manage the expanding federal government are largely removed from the ebbs and flows of the private economy, in which the middle class is struggling. Indeed, the political class seems more interested in expanding government than expanding the economy.

The increasing centralization of government power also erodes the independence of the middle class. With federal power reaching into more and more areas, political decisions once made in local middle-class communities are now being made in Washington, D.C.

The massive administrative state rests on the belief that only an expert elite can adequately govern the country. This belief envisions the average person not as a sovereign voice within American democracy but as a dependent client of government—something to justify the growing power of government agencies. Under progressive paternalism, the role of the individual is not to act but to be acted upon. Big-government advocates resist giving the middle class control over their Social Security accounts, despite the fact that the government-run Social Security system is going broke. They resist giving individuals control over the structure of their health care, even though nearly every assurance they made about the ACA proved false. They resist giving families their choice of schools, even though the public schools assigned to their children are failing.

Work is the pathway to the middle class and to independence, but government policies often exert a depressing effect on work. For instance, according to the Congressional Budget Office, the ACA reduced incentives to work so much that "the labor force is projected to be about 2 million full-time-equivalent workers smaller in 2025 than it would have been otherwise." In other words, the ACA created incentives for working-age, able-bodied adults to choose government dependence over self-reliance.

The integrity of work has been one of the most serious casualties of the big-government culture of recent years. Nearly a decade after the recession began, the economy still employed millions fewer full-time workers than it did in 2007. Tens of millions of working-age Americans were working part-time involuntarily or had dropped out of the workforce.

The percentage of adult Americans out of the labor force hit a thirty-eight-year high in 2015; two years later it was only a few tenths of a point lower. High-wage industries lost a million positions in the decade after 2007, and the highest job growth occurred in low-wage, low-skill, part-time industries. The trend of declining labor-force participation was particularly pronounced among the working-age poor, with three out of five not working at all.

The decline in job creation corresponded with a decline in new business start-ups, which in many industries neared a thirty-five-year low. A 2016 survey by the National Federation of Independent Business reported that worries about "unreasonable government regulations" had shot to second on the list of small businesses' concerns, behind only the rising costs of health insurance—another consequence of government interventionism.

BIG GOVERNMENT AND INEQUALITY

Many economists claim that the gap between rich and poor is at its widest point since record keeping began nearly a half century ago. This gap widened throughout the economic recovery. According to the Federal Reserve, from 2010 to 2013 only the households at the very top of the income ladder saw gains; families in the bottom 40 percent saw their incomes decline, while household incomes in the middle stagnated.

Although the wealthiest Americans experienced substantial gains after the 2008 recession, the real incomes of poor and middle-class households declined significantly. Moreover, the supply of midwage jobs shrank proportionally more than that of jobs at the top or bottom.

A state-by-state analysis shows that states with big-government policies have larger income gaps than do states whose more limited governments follow growth-oriented policies. So, at the minimum, redistributionist policies like raising tax rates or the minimum wage fail to achieve greater income equality. And at worst, such policies actually worsen the inequality by dampening economic opportunity and mobility.

The minimum wage is no growth measure. It is a government dictate that fails to address the much bigger problem of economic stagnation. Raising the minimum wage benefits those lucky individuals who keep their minimum-wage jobs, but it decreases the number of such jobs in the future. And it may end up keeping minimum-wage workers at their current wage level for longer periods of time without salary raises. Furthermore, since the holders of minimum-wage jobs may not be from low-income families—they may be the children or spouses of primary earners who make higher incomes—the minimum wage may not be effective at helping poor families.

The problem with big-government responses to inequality is that they require government to be the primary agent or focus. All that really happens is that government ends up bigger and more powerful. For instance, a frequent big-government approach to inequality is to intensify government-directed wealth-redistribution programs. A better response, and one proven to boost mobility, is to increase innovation, which will increase economic opportunity, and then to provide a better and more flexible education system, which will equip individuals to take advantage of those new opportunities. But a huge barrier to better-educated individuals is the unresponsive, monopolistic public school system. And a huge barrier to innovation is a bureaucratic government that increases regulations and otherwise helps entrenched corporate incumbents block the entry of competitors offering new products.

Debates about inequality frequently ignore these realities. As is so often the case, the advocates of big government focus on their noble intentions when what really matters are results. In the end, big government doesn't help the poor and working-class Americans who are the supposed beneficiaries of federal largesse. Instead, the political elites get more powerful and the wealthy get wealthier.

Point #4

←——→

BIG GOVERNMENT BECOMES ITS OWN END

The advocates for big government often take a simplistic approach to social problems. Since any problem can be solved by a government program, then a new or expanded government program is itself a sign that the problem has been addressed.

Government, then, stops being a means for addressing social problems and becomes an end in itself. Under this approach, all focus goes to the government—e.g., how much money government is spending, or how big the scope of its programs is.

Lost in all this is the problem itself. Rarely is there an analysis of whether government is actually helping anyone other than the bureaucrats it employs. Nor is there any analysis of whether the burden government places on other people—through taxes and regulations—is overcome by the actual benefits it is delivering to those who may really need them.

GOVERNMENT SIZE BECOMES THE PROXY FOR ANY SOCIAL REMEDY

Once government has grown large enough to possess its own power base, its primary aim is to perpetuate itself. Bureaucrats become a class bent on serving their own interests.

Take the Veterans Health Administration scandal that exploded in 2014. This federal agency, part of the Department of Veterans Affairs (VA), is charged with providing medical care to those who have served our country in the armed services. It turned out that VA hospitals were making military veterans wait for service well beyond the targeted fourteen-day period. Some veterans died while on the waiting list, and some hospitals falsified records to make it look like they were meeting their targets. The VA system paid out $200 million in wrongful-death settlements over a decade. Instead of being disciplined for mismanagement, VA officials received generous bonuses.

The scandal demonstrated how the VA employees themselves—not our nation's veterans—became the agency's most important constituency. And this constituency was committed to government perpetuation. The union representing VA employees gave 97 percent of its political

DID YOU KNOW?

In the first fifty years of the "War on Poverty," the federal government spent *triple* what the United States had spent on all military wars since the American Revolution.

donations at the national level and 100 percent at the state level to candidates committed to big government.

The field of education provides another good example of how government, through the public school system and its teachers' unions, uses the power of its education monopoly to sustain that monopoly, even at the expense of children. School-choice programs and charter schools come under attack not because they are bad at educating children but because they are good at it, which threatens the government's monopoly. Private schools and public charter schools graduate more students, send more students to college, and achieve higher test scores, while at the same time educating students at a lower cost, than does the public school system. They can do so largely because they do not have to abide by all the rules aimed at protecting government employees.

Nonetheless, under a government-as-proxy approach, the solution to education problems is simply to increase the government education budget. And when that budget has been increased, the problem is said to have been addressed.

As an example of government's refusal to consider nongovernmental solutions to social issues, the Wisconsin Institute for Law and Liberty in 2017 reported on the

Milwaukee Public Schools' ongoing resistance to selling its vacant buildings to charter schools or private schools. Even though the vacant school buildings cost taxpayers $1.4 million each year to maintain, the city and the school board repeatedly rejected attempts by Saint Marcus School, a private Lutheran school that participated in Milwaukee's choice program, to purchase one of the vacant buildings. A Milwaukee official informed Saint Marcus that "city policy does not contemplate the sale of city controlled real estate for use by private schools affiliated with the Milwaukee Parental Choice Program." This was despite the fact that Saint Marcus had offered more than $1 million to purchase the abandoned property (which had a fair market value of $423,500) and would have invested more than $5 million into the neighborhood and hired hundreds of staff. Most important, Saint Marcus would have provided six hundred children with a top-quality education: even though 90 percent of its students came from low-income families, more than 91 percent of Saint Marcus students graduated from high school in four years or fewer.

The Wisconsin state legislature then stepped in. In 2015 the legislature approved the so-called Surplus Property Law, a budget provision that forced the city of Milwaukee to sell vacant buildings to private or charter schools. But over the next two years, the city sold only one such property, as the Milwaukee Public Schools refused to list many of its vacant buildings. The Wisconsin Institute for Law and Liberty concluded, "City politicians—those who prefer the interests of government employees over those of families—have consistently failed to comply with the Surplus Property Law and frustrated its purpose."

The Milwaukee Public Schools board president betrayed the public sector's fear of competition when he said that selling vacant buildings to choice schools would be like "asking the Coca-Cola Company to turn over its facilities to Pepsi so Pepsi can expand and compete with the Coca-Cola Company."

THE FAILINGS OF BIG-GOVERNMENT POVERTY PROGRAMS

Antipoverty policy in the United States presents an acute example of how government has become a proxy for social remedies. Ever since the Great Society programs of the 1960s, big-government advocates have offered the same solution to America's poverty problems: more government programs and spending.

The big-government antipoverty agenda primarily advances the reach of government. The poor become a pawn, a justification for bigger government. This is why big-government advocates oppose many reform proposals—because those proposals do not permanently enlarge government.

In 2014 the Heritage Foundation reported that in the half century since President Lyndon Johnson announced the War on Poverty, the federal government had spent more than $22 trillion (measured in 2012 dollars) fighting this "war." Adjusted for inflation, this spending amounted to *triple* what the United States spent on all military wars since the American Revolution. Inflation-adjusted government transfers for social-welfare programs soared more than tenfold between 1964 and 2013.

But all this spending did little for the poor.

The poverty rate in 2017 was about the same as it was fifty years earlier. The rate fell much more rapidly before President Johnson instituted the Great Society than at any point afterward: in the seven years between 1959 and 1966, according to the Census Bureau, the percentage of people living in poverty dropped by about a third, from 22.4 percent to 14.7 percent. Even in the years following the record federal stimulus program of 2009, the poverty rate hovered around 15 percent—slightly higher than it was in 1966. And the poverty rates for children under eighteen and for working-age people (eighteen to sixty-four) were actually higher than in 1966. If a person today is born in poverty, that person is as likely to stay poor as they were fifty years ago.

In 2016, forty-four million Americans received food-stamp aid from the federal government, an increase of almost 50 percent since the massive economic-stimulus spending of the Obama era. In other words, one in seven citizens in the wealthiest economy on earth now relied on food aid from the government.

As of 2013, the federal government ran more than eighty different antipoverty programs at a cost of more than $900 billion per year.

The ineffectiveness of these programs can be seen by dividing the $900 billion in federal spending on anti-poverty programs by the forty-three million people in poverty. If the government decided to eliminate these programs and simply distribute a cash payment to everyone in America living below the poverty line, it would send each family of four $75,000—almost triple the federal poverty line for that family. In other words, everyone would be statistically lifted out of poverty.

Government absorbs far too much money in maintaining its own bureaucracy. The big-government approach to poverty simply isn't an effective way to help the poor.

Once again, government has become the end, not the means.

THE DEPENDENCY TRAP

Waste and inefficiency are not the only problems with the federal government's antipoverty measures. Another issue is that what the government does dole out to the poor ends up trapping them in dependency, rather than giving them the resources to climb out of poverty and advance their life's condition.

Historically, America tried to avoid dependence on government relief. Even the New Deal didn't permanently enshrine dependency. Recovery from the Great Depression occurred hand-in-hand with a great decline in the number of people on public aid. In 1951 the Social Security commissioner reported that just 3.8 percent of Americans were receiving public aid, down from 11.5 percent in 1940.

But the Great Society programs of the 1960s led to dramatic changes in government-induced dependency. Writing in 2014, on the Great Society's fiftieth anniversary, American Enterprise Institute scholar Nicholas Eberstadt observed:

Dependence on government relief, in its many modern versions, is more widespread today, and possibly also more habitual, than at any time in our history. To make matters much worse, such aid has become integral to financing lifestyles and behavioral patterns plainly destructive to our commonwealth—and on a scale far vaster than could have been imagined in an era before such antipoverty aid was all but unconditionally available.

Any humane and civilized society should have a safety net to prevent vulnerable people from sliding into abject poverty. The problem occurs when safety nets turn into traps—keeping people permanently dependent on government subsidies.

President Johnson proclaimed that the War on Poverty would not create such traps. On signing War on Poverty legislation, LBJ said: "Our American answer to poverty is not to make the poor more secure in their poverty but to reach down and to help them lift themselves out of the ruts of poverty and move with the large majority along the high road of hope and prosperity. The days of the dole in our country are numbered."

This prediction has proved wrong.

Dependency shot up in the wake of the War on Poverty. The proportion of men twenty and older who are employed has steadily dropped, falling from 80.6 percent in 1964 to 67.6 percent fifty years later. The proportion of adult men in the labor force either working or looking for work likewise declined, from 84.2 percent to 71.9 percent.

IGNORING THE CAUSES OF POVERTY

The War on Poverty agenda reflected the belief that a stronger central government, acting through agencies of expertise, could fix the technocratic problem of poverty as revealed by statistical income gaps among various population groups.

But government programs have failed to solve the problem, largely because they have never addressed the fundamental causes of poverty.

One root cause of poverty is a lack of work, so the key to ending poverty is putting people to work. But too often, government social-welfare programs discourage work by making government benefits more attractive than work or by penalizing the rewards of work. Take, for example, the situation of a single mother with one child who earns the minimum wage and receives food stamps, Medicaid, and housing assistance. If she takes a job that pays three dollars more per hour, she will keep only ten cents of every extra dollar she makes, after tax hikes and benefit cuts. Therefore, taking that higher-paying job turns out to yield virtually zero rewards. The War on Poverty and its successor programs have offered able-bodied people alternatives to work in the form of welfare.

The federal disability program likewise discourages work. Even though medical care has advanced tremendously over the past fifty years, and even though the physical demands of workplace labor have drastically diminished, the number of disability claimants receiving payment for back pain or other musculoskeletal problems increased nearly fourfold from 1961 to 2015.

Another root cause of poverty is behavioral. Countless studies repeat the same message: that poverty in America is often intertwined with social pathologies. Drug or alcohol abuse, criminality, domestic violence, family breakdown—all these factors have a strong correlation with poverty.

People who marry before having children, avoid substance abuse, graduate from high school, stay out of jail, and hold even minimum-wage jobs for at least a year virtually never end up living in poverty. But work begins with employability, and behavioral problems can prevent a person from getting a job. One thing the federal government has never been able to do is to teach behavioral lessons or character values to those who most need them.

> **THOUGHTS ON BIG GOVERNMENT**
>
> "The politics of kindness is about validating oneself rather than helping others, which means the proper response to suffering is always, 'We need to do more,' and never, 'We need to do what we're already doing better and smarter.'"
>
> —William Voegeli, *Imprimis*

Even back during the 1960s, some government policymakers understood the limits of big-government approaches to fighting poverty. An early study by Walter Heller, chair of President John F. Kennedy's Council of Economic Advisers, warned that "government welfare unwittingly contributes to broken homes and illegitimacy." This warning anticipated the well-known

Moynihan Report, which in 1965 cautioned that welfare expansion would destroy black families.

In fact, social pathologies have become significantly worse since the War on Poverty began. The out-of-wedlock birth rate for African Americans soared from 25 percent then to 70 percent a half century later. America's overall out-of-wedlock birth rate increased sixfold. And by eroding marriage, the welfare state has made many Americans less capable of self-support.

Advocates of big government often express their agenda as the "politics of kindness." By implication, then, the advocates of more limited government are the advocates of a politics of cruelty, greed, and callousness. But kindness goes far beyond just advocating that the government get bigger and spend more. Kindness looks to whether fellow human beings are improving their lives. To big-government advocates, it is as if noble intentions are most important.

If big-government advocates were truly concerned about improving the lives of the poor, one would think they would scrutinize the effectiveness of the social-welfare state, which is now the biggest thing that government does. And yet they resist such scrutiny. In fact, they attack anyone who seeks to evaluate results or who proposes reforms to federal antipoverty programs (or any other federal programs, for that matter).

Inflation-adjusted per capita federal spending on the welfare state increased 254 percent from 1977 to 2013, all without an appreciable reduction in poverty. And yet anyone who questions the social-welfare state is labeled cruel or mean-spirited. The only response big-government advocates can offer to persistent poverty is to say that government should spend even more, regardless of the decades of evidence showing that this approach doesn't work well.

BIG GOVERNMENT CAN BETRAY THE POOR

Perhaps the most troubling aspect of the "politics of kindness" is that big-government programs can actually *hurt* the people they are supposed to help.

Take the 2008 housing crisis and subsequent recession, which stemmed from a vast oversupply of unsustainable mortgages on the market. These mortgages were issued to people who had bought homes beyond their financial capacity. Subsequently, those substandard mortgages were packaged and resold to unsuspecting investors. When housing prices fell and foreclosures mounted, the housing market crashed, along with the subprime-mortgage market, leading to the Great Recession. The root of the crisis was that many of the subprime mortgages did not meet the most basic underwriting standards. So the question becomes, how did such mortgages come into existence?

The answer reaches back to policies the federal government adopted during Bill Clinton's administration. President Clinton and his economic team sought what was, on the face of it, a laudable goal: to expand home ownership in America. But to achieve that goal, federal regulators pushed banks into disregarding traditional underwriting standards so low-income borrowers could receive mortgages for which they previously couldn't qualify. The federal government also forced Fannie Mae and Freddie Mac to keep increasing the percentage of "affordable-housing" loans they made: the quota jumped from 30 percent in 1992 to 50 percent in 2000, as Phil Gramm and Mike Solon noted in the *Wall Street Journal*. Of course, a big push for such programs came from the construction, real-estate, and banking lobbies.

It was government that led the charge into subprime lending, flooding the market with substandard mortgages, and it was government that wound up holding the vast majority of high-risk loans in the United States. By 2008, government agencies like Fannie Mae and Freddie Mac held more than three-quarters of all subprime mortgages. When these substandard mortgages went into default, the poor were hurt in two ways. First, during the housing crash that resulted, they lost the homes into which they had been lured, along with any equity that they had put into those homes. Second, when the Great Recession followed, they lost their jobs and income.

As Democrat Barney Frank admitted in 2010, "It was a great mistake to push lower-income people into housing they couldn't afford and couldn't really handle once they had it."

The urban housing projects that began in the 1960s represent another well-intended government program that betrayed the poor. These massive housing developments, spawned by big government's approach to the War on Poverty, included complexes such as Cabrini-Green and Robert Taylor Homes in Chicago, which crowded young children, single-parent families, and the elderly into high-rise buildings with hardened criminals, drug dealers, and gang members. The projects became notorious for shootings, gang wars, drug trafficking, and prostitution. Finally, in the 1990s and early 2000s, the federal government ordered the demolition of these and thousands of other such housing projects, testifying to the utter and tragic failures of the developments.

The government started out with a noble goal—to provide housing to the urban poor—but in pursuing this goal it sentenced countless children and families to dangerous, desperate existences.

Big-government programs can also rob the poor of much-needed resources. In New York City, for instance, government officials banned all food donations to homeless shelters—possibly the most traditional example of private giving—because the city could not assess the food's salt, fat, and fiber content. And at the national level, the Department of Health and Human Services threatened to impose a multimillion-dollar fine on Little Sisters of the Poor, a Catholic order of nuns that helps the elderly, because their religious faith does not allow them to provide employees with contraception.

As Philip Howard pointed out in *The Rule of Nobody: Saving America from Dead Laws and Broken Government*, a soup kitchen in New Jersey served the poor and elderly three hundred meals per day for twenty-six years—until the health department shut it down. Churchgoers made the meals in their homes, and state law required that every preparation site be examined. But since the department could not inspect every private kitchen, it shut down the whole program instead.

As a result of these government policies, the poor lose the personalized care that characterizes private giving, as well as the human bonds that tie them to the community. Studies repeatedly show that personal attention and supportive relationships reduce poverty better than financial assistance alone. By crowding out private help, government programs deny the poor these essential relationships, leaving them with a handout but no human hand to help pull them out of poverty.

Of course, even the government's monetary handouts don't always reach the neediest. For instance, a 2012 study by the Congressional Budget Office (CBO) found that over the previous thirty years, the share of government transfer payments going to the poorest quintile of Americans declined from 50 percent to 35 percent.

The Special Supplemental Nutrition Program for Women, Infants, and Children (WIC), a federal nutrition program aimed at low-income beneficiaries, has over time been channeled to recipients with significantly higher incomes. In 2014 nearly one-quarter of WIC recipients lived in families with annual incomes exceeding 185 percent of the poverty line and hence should not have qualified under the program.

Another government program purporting to benefit the poor, Oregon Promise, offered free community college. But it channeled 60 percent of its spending to students from upper-middle-class and rich families.

The Social Security system hurts the poor and working class in various ways. As a share of income, the payroll tax is the largest tax paid by most workers. And yet a 2017 CBO report projected that the United States could maintain current Social Security benefits and cover the expected funding shortfalls "only if payroll taxes were raised immediately and permanently by about 4.5 percent of taxable payroll." Without these tax increases, which will fall most heavily on the working class, benefits will have to be cut if the system is to avoid insolvency. And because working Americans have grown dependent on all the promised entitlements, they are the ones most vulnerable to insolvency or benefit cutbacks.

The changing demographics of food-stamp recipients provide another sign that federal antipoverty programs are not working. The Supplemental Nutrition Assistance Program (SNAP) helps low-income individuals and households. Previously, children and the elderly made up the majority of food-stamp recipients. But the number of nonworking, nondisabled, working-age recipients has risen rapidly, to the point that nonelderly adults now account for a majority of SNAP recipients. Rather than promoting self-sufficiency, SNAP has expanded dependency and encouraged working-age adults not to work.

Between 2008 and 2013, the number of SNAP recipients grew nearly 69 percent. (By contrast, the poverty rate increased just 16.5 percent during the same period.) A key factor in this rise was the decision that many states made to waive a work requirement for recipients.

By bringing more beneficiaries into SNAP, the government expands its reach at the cost of human dependency. As of 2017, more than half of SNAP users had been in the program for longer than five years, which suggests that most recipients were using this federal assistance as a permanent source of income, not as a temporary safety net.

The dependency-fostering aspect of SNAP becomes further evident in those instances when states reinstalled work requirements. When Kansas stopped the work waiver in 2013, the number of able-bodied adults with dependents receiving SNAP benefits dropped 75 percent. And those who left the program saw their income increase 125 percent on average.

The Kansas example shows how destructive big-government programs can be to individual independence and self-sufficiency. Yet the vast majority of the federal government's eighty means-tested welfare programs do not include a work requirement. The real victim is not the taxpayer who funds those programs—it is the individual recipient who is discouraged from building a better life for herself.

Too often, however, big-government advocates don't take stock of these victims. This is what happens when policymakers lose sight of the problem they are supposed to be solving and focus all their attention on the size and scope of government.

Point #5

←——→

BIG GOVERNMENT BACKFIRES

A rule of common sense states that when something grows too big, it grows unworkable and even abusive. In many respects, government has reached that point. And yet the federal government continues to expand itself.

Public-sector unions, for instance, have emerged as a powerful internal force for government expansion. As the federal government employs more people, public-sector unions grow larger and have more political power to lobby for bigger government. These public-sector unions become a built-in political force for an expanding federal government. During the 2016 presidential election, 95 percent of the political donations from fourteen agencies went to Hillary Clinton, a candidate committed to big government.

According to its advocates, the big-government entitlement state provides safety and security to hundreds of millions of poor and working-class individuals. But as the federal debt reaches unsustainable levels, the financial futures of poor and working-class Americans become increasingly vulnerable—vulnerable to the federal government's failure to fulfill all its shaky promises.

In 1962, before the Great Society started, mandatory spending constituted only 30 percent of the federal budget. By 2016, the figure had passed 60 percent. But as mandatory spending rises, powered by Social Security and Medicare, there is less and less room for such discretionary but necessary programs as defense and education. And as the rest of society pushes for more discretionary spending, entitlement programs will come under pressure.

Interest payments from the ballooning federal debt are projected to exceed all spending on Social Security, Medicare, and national defense combined. When that happens, entitlements will be cut, and/or big tax hikes will be implemented—tax increases from which the rich will find ways to escape, leaving working Americans to bear the biggest burden.

The more government tries to do, the more it unduly extends itself, and the more it fails. Government, as the founders concluded, must be limited to be effective. When government grows to unforeseen lengths, it extends itself beyond its abilities. Failures occur more frequently. And the more government fails, the less the public trusts it.

Recall from the introduction the survey data showing the steep decline in Americans' faith in the federal government. In a 2017 poll by the Pew Research Center, only 20 percent of Americans said they trusted the federal government to do what's right "just about always" or "most of the time." Back in 1964, on the eve of the Great Society, 77 percent of Americans expressed such trust.

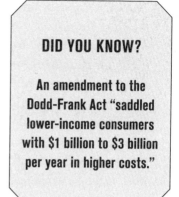

DID YOU KNOW?

An amendment to the Dodd-Frank Act "saddled lower-income consumers with $1 billion to $3 billion per year in higher costs."

In 2015, when Gallup asked how much trust and confidence Americans had in the federal government to handle domestic problems, 61 percent answered "not very much" or "none at all." That figure was a record high for this question, which Gallup began asking in 1972. Gallup also asks Americans what they believe poses the greatest threat to the future of the country: big government, big business, or big labor. Back in 1965, only 35 percent said big government; in 2013, big government received a record-high response rate of 72 percent.

A loss of confidence in the federal government should not surprise anyone. This is what happens when government grows unwieldy, ineffective, and unaccountable. To the government expanders, bigger is always better. But the reality is that when it comes to government, bigness backfires.

WHEN BIGNESS LEADS TO ABUSE

As the framers foresaw, a government without effective limits ultimately succumbs to abusive behavior. And just the past few years have brought a host of examples of abuse by the federal government.

There is no more glaring example of government abuse than the scandal in which the Internal Revenue Service (IRS) targeted political opponents of the administration. Even though no agency is less forgiving about individual record keeping than the IRS, the IRS claimed that information requested by investigators had disappeared from its electronic data files. The IRS expects taxpayers to keep up to seven years of personal tax records but could not keep even six months of employee emails.

The IRS brushed off the targeting scandal investigation, expecting Congress to believe that it had innocently destroyed relevant evidence. In a show of arrogance, the head of the IRS even tried to use the scandal to pressure Congress into appropriating more money to the agency.

But congressional investigating committees and the U.S. Treasury inspector general for tax administration discovered that the IRS's targeting of conservative groups was real. In 2013 the IRS commissioner was forced to resign when investigators learned that he had known IRS employees were targeting political groups but that he hadn't admitted his knowledge in congressional testimony.

An investigation of the IRS's Cincinati office, out of which the targeting of conservative groups largely took place, found that during the 2012 election season more than 90 percent of all political donations traceable from that office went to candidates who advocated for bigger government.

The Veterans Health Administration scandal, discussed in the previous chapter, offers another case study in government abuse. The VA routinely subjected eligible veterans to excessive waits for health care and then covered it up through falsified records. The Phoenix VA Hospital reported that the average waiting time for medical appointments was 24 days; the real waiting time, according to the VA inspector general's report, was 115 days. The inspector general found within the VA a widespread conspiracy to keep veterans off the official waiting lists.

The scandal did not occur because of a lack of money. The VA's budget had more than tripled over just a dozen years, from $45 billion in 2000 to $154 billion in 2012.

The VA scandal illustrates one of the fundamental flaws of highly centralized public health-care systems that do not permit meaningful pricing and do not allow for competition among care providers: they can respond to demand pressures only by manipulating waiting lines. Expanding federal control over health care was a prominent political focus after 2008. But the VA scandal has discredited big government more than any abstract argument ever could.

FAILING THE COMMON PERSON: THE HEALTH-CARE DEBACLE

The whole federal takeover of health care was riddled with failures. The Affordable Care Act (ACA), one of the most far-reaching pieces of legislation in history, began with grandiose promises of providing affordable health insurance to all Americans. In reality, the ACA, by injecting the federal government into every aspect of health care, dragged down both the individual and society.

The rollout of the HealthCare.gov website was a disaster. It was such a mess that the day the site went live, only six people in the entire country were able to sign up for health plans. A year and a half after the HealthCare.gov launch, the Associated Press revealed that the government site was releasing personal health data to dozens of third-party websites. The Office of Inspector General for the Department of Health and Human Services discovered that federal officials in charge of the rollout "received 18 written warnings that the mammoth project was mismanaged and off course but never considered postponing its launch," in the words of the *Washington Post*.

The investigators' report painted a portrait of federal officials who failed to grasp the sheer scope of the project, who were disorganized and took a fragmented approach, and who repeatedly ignored problems. This portrait could apply to big government in general.

In testimony before the U.S. Senate, the nonpartisan Government Accountability Office (GAO) stated in July 2015 that the biggest threat to ACA implementation remained government ineptitude. The GAO revealed, for instance, that during its investigation it had little difficulty enrolling fictitious applicants on the federal exchange and obtaining subsidies for them.

ACA implementation brought many other problems. The oft-repeated promises of "If you like your doctor, you can keep your doctor" and "If you like your health-care plan, you can keep your health-care plan" quickly proved false. Health-care co-ops went out of business at an alarming rate. Individual insurance plans were canceled. The consolidation of doctors and hospitals diminished individual access to doctors. And then, because the ACA did not always work or meet its deadlines, the administration gave selected groups waivers from various ACA mandates.

Moreover, the people who enrolled in the ACA exchanges were sicker and more heavily subsidized than had been anticipated. Many healthy uninsured people chose to pay a fine and go without coverage, which led to increased premiums charged on the exchanges.

At the centerpiece of the ACA scheme were twenty-three insurance co-ops—government-sponsored nonprofits that were supposed to increase competition among insurers, expand the number of health-insurance companies available, and lower prices to the consumer. But they proved to be a debacle. In 2015 every one of the ACA's co-ops lost money, and by the end of 2016, sixteen of them had folded. Their $1.3 billion in federal loans will probably never be paid back. All the enrollees in those failed co-ops had to try to find alternative coverage.

ACA boosters promised that the law would reduce overall health-care costs. In fact, the ACA made health insurance more expensive. A headline in the January 10, 2016, *New York Times* stated, "Insurers Say Costs Are Climbing as More Enroll Past Health Act Deadline." An article in the November 19, 2015, *Wall Street Journal*, titled "Rising Rates Pose Challenge to Health Law," noted that many people signing up for policies under the ACA faced higher premiums, fewer doctors, and skimpier coverage.

In 2017 health-insurance premiums under the ACA rose on average 25 percent, according to the Department of Health and Human Services. Premiums rose in every state except Indiana and Massachusetts. Rates in Arizona increased 116 percent; in Oklahoma, 69 percent; in Tennessee, 63 percent; and in Pennsylvania, 53 percent. According to a 2017 HHS report, twenty-four states saw individual health-insurance premiums double since 2013.

In lobbying for the ACA, supporters claimed that the typical family would see a yearly savings of $2,500 in their health costs. But average family premiums for employer health coverage rose from $13,375 in 2009 to $17,545 in 2015. Data from the Centers for Medicare and Medicaid Services project that total per capita health-insurance spending will rise from $7,786 in 2016 to $11,681 in 2024.

Under the ACA, health-care costs soared for the young, who saw premium increases of up to 44 percent. Moreover, the ACA prohibited minimum-coverage plans that are especially appropriate for young people, who generally need or want only basic coverage through a limited benefit plan.

According to the Kaiser Family Foundation, the average health-insurance deductible for all workers increased 67 percent from 2010 to 2015. An average family of four saw their total health costs, including premiums and out-of-pocket expenses, grow by 43 percent over that five-year period. Relative to incomes, health premiums were twice as large as they were in the early 2000s.

Another aspect of the ACA, the so-called Cadillac tax, has hurt working people. It was originally advertised as imposing a 40 percent excise tax only on high-value employer-provided health benefits. But approximately 175 million Americans are enrolled in employer-sponsored health plans, meaning that the Cadillac tax has more reach than advertised. Employers understandably do not want to pay the steep excise tax, so the tax creates incentives for them to reduce benefits or perhaps even stop providing health-care benefits altogether, thus forcing their employees to migrate towards the ACA's exchanges. In many cases, employers would find it cheaper to pay the fine for not complying with the ACA mandate to offer full-time employees health-insurance coverage.

Worse, under the ACA, the thresholds at which the tax kicked in for individuals and families were indexed to overall inflation, not to the faster-rising health-care costs. Like the dreaded alternative minimum tax, which was designed to apply only to the wealthiest Americans in 1969 but now impacts millions of households with incomes above $83,400, the Cadillac tax will steadily pull more and more Americans into its net. Although the Cadillac tax started out hitting only 8 percent of insurance plans, a 2014 Towers Watson survey revealed that 82 percent of employers expected to incur a Cadillac tax liability by 2023.

The ACA also introduced "incentives to change the workweek," according to University of Chicago economist Casey Mulligan. In a 2014 research paper titled "The Affordable Care Act and the New Economics of Part-Time Work," Mulligan cited three ACA provisions that created perverse incentives. The first and "most obvious," he wrote, was the employer mandate, which required companies

THOUGHTS ON BIG GOVERNMENT

"Since the passage of the Dodd-Frank Act the pace at which community banks have lost market share is nearly double what it was during the crisis."

—Marshall Lux and Robert Greene of Harvard University's John F. Kennedy School of Government, *The State and Fate of Community Banking*

that did not offer full-time employees health insurance to pay a penalty of $2,000 per employee. "Naturally, a penalty on full-time employment can be expected to lead to less full-time employment," Mulligan said.

The ACA imposed the employer mandate on companies with fifty or more full-time employees working more than thirty hours a week. Sure enough, the percentage of employees working between thirty-one and thirty-four hours per week dropped from 7.7 percent in 2009, before ACA passed, to 6.6 percent in 2013. Meanwhile, the percentage of part-timers working twenty-five to twenty-nine hours a week increased from 9.7 percent to 11.1 percent.

In addition to this "explicit tax" were two "implicit" taxes: one on full-time employment and the other on earnings. The implicit tax on full-time employment stemmed from the fact that someone who qualified for employer-offered insurance coverage wasn't eligible to receive subsidies on the ACA's exchanges. The implicit tax on earnings resulted because the law gave lower subsidies to those with higher incomes, effectively penalizing individuals who worked longer hours and earned more. These two provisions created obvious incentives for people to work less. In one example Mulligan cited, a person would take home more net pay if she earned $37,700 per year in a part-time position than if she earned $52,000 working full time. Such an arrangement encourages government dependency and makes it harder for workers to save for their own retirement through 401(k)s and similar vehicles.

In short, the ACA encouraged employers to lay off full-time employees or cut them back to part time, and it also discouraged people from seeking full-time work.

Little wonder, then, that the Congressional Budget Office projected that the ACA would remove the equivalent of two million full-time workers from the labor force by 2025. Suffering the most will be lower-income workers, whose jobs are disproportionately shed or cut back, and who most feel the burden of rising health-care costs and reduced benefits.

FAILING THE COMMON PERSON: FINANCIAL AND ECONOMIC REGULATIONS

As previously discussed, financial regulations like the Dodd-Frank Act breed crony capitalism and create incentives for big business to get even bigger. Not surprisingly, then, they work against the interests of the common person.

Most new employment comes from small business, especially entrepreneurial start-ups, but new regulatory costs place a disproportionately high burden on small businesses. Such a burden has resulted from Dodd-Frank rules that have escalated costs for small banks and applied the kind of lending standards to small banks that make it difficult for them to finance start-ups.

Dodd Frank has hurt low-income individuals in other ways. Banks drastically cut back on free checking accounts and increased monthly maintenance fees on other accounts. According to Todd Zywicki of the Law and Economics Center and Julian Morris of the Reason Foundation, this piece of Dodd-Frank "saddled lower-income consumers with $1 billion to $3 billion per year in higher costs" in the form of increased bank fees and restricted access to bank services.

The real tragedy to working Americans arises because these costs and burdens were unjustified. Dodd-Frank, passed in 2010 and falsely proclaimed as a necessary remedy for the causes of the 2008 recession, did not even address the true causes of the crisis. All it really did was to further expand the federal government's regulatory reach in ways that are still unknown.

Along with more specifically directed federal regulatory schemes like Dodd-Frank, massive federal spending programs exert a regressive effect on the common person. The $831 billion stimulus program adopted in 2009, as previously mentioned, failed to stimulate employment, spur income growth in the working or middle class, or reduce poverty appreciably. Instead it plunged the country deeper into debt and led to the Federal Reserve's quantitative easing, the main effect of which was to create a financial windfall for Wall Street.

Like the ACA, many government social-welfare programs create perverse incentives, leading people to work fewer hours or even to leave the labor force entirely. One economic study showed that low-skilled immigrants are far more willing than low-skilled natives to move in response to rising unemployment. One key factor here is that immigrants are far less likely than natives to be eligible for unemployment insurance and other local safety-net programs. In other words, government dependence suppresses the drive to seek out new opportunities.

Rent-control laws also harm the poor and vulnerable. These laws inhibit developers from building new rental housing, which leads to housing shortages and forces the poor into overcrowded units. Under rent-control schemes, landlords also reduce their maintenance expenditures, resulting in lower-quality housing.

Real-estate-development restrictions likewise disadvantage the poor. By decreasing the supply of affordable housing, these restrictions allow slumlords to jack up rents even on their dilapidated properties. Perhaps not surprisingly, housing shortages are most acute in liberal cities. UCLA economist Matthew Kahn found that the higher a city's liberal vote share, the fewer housing permits it issues. The irony of Kahn's findings is that several of California's large, liberal cities have enacted local minimum wages that are higher than the state's minimum wage, on the ground that housing costs are too high for low-wage workers to afford. But housing costs are so high largely because the cities have adopted development restrictions.

So a vicious circle results. Government raises minimum wages to combat the increasing costs of housing, which increased regulation has caused, and then the increased minimum wages decrease the supply of low-income jobs, which makes it even harder for the poor to afford housing.

THE FALLOUT FROM HIGHER-EDUCATION POLICIES

Big-government intervention has backfired in higher education as well. As a result of the federal student-loan program, college costs have skyrocketed.

Progressive politicians often bemoan ever-increasing college tuition costs and then call for additional federal spending to make college more affordable. The problem is that college tuitions have soared largely *because* federal money is so readily available. Colleges have responded by doing what subsidized industries generally do: raising prices to capture the subsidy.

Thirty years ago, Secretary of Education William J. Bennett wrote a *New York Times* op-ed in which he challenged college administrators who claimed that they needed to raise tuition in the face of government cutbacks. On the contrary, Bennett said: "increases in financial aid in recent years have enabled colleges and universities blithely to raise their tuitions, confident that Federal loan subsidies would help cushion the increase."

The past three decades have shown the so-called Bennett Hypothesis to be correct. Although the federal student loan program is portrayed as helping students cope with rising college costs, that program has been a major contributor to the escalating costs of higher education. Federal spending on college aid has increased approximately seventeenfold since 1970. And in a July 2015 report, the Federal Reserve Bank of New York found a causal connection between government spending and tuition levels. Before the late 1970s, federal financial aid programs were modest in size. Correspondingly, annual tuition increases were roughly one percentage point more than overall inflation. But since 1978, during the era of rapidly growing federal loan programs, annual tuition increases have outpaced inflation by a factor of three to four.

Tuition at public four-year colleges nearly quadrupled between 1980 and 2016. Tuition costs grew by 80 percent in just the ten years between 2003 and 2013, whereas the consumer price index increased only 26 percent.

To pay these rising tuition costs, students have gone into severe debt. As of the end of 2016, Americans owed more than $1.3 *trillion* in student loan debt, close to double the total American credit card debt. The outstanding debt load nearly tripled in just a decade.

The delinquency rate among those making student-loan payments reached more than 11 percent in 2016, nearly double the 2003 rate. According to the Department of Education, 43 percent of the twenty-two million Americans with federal student loans were not making payments as of January 1, 2016.

The federal student-loan program can entice young people to incur unmanageable debt to fund financially untested endeavors. In 2012, 681 public colleges had graduation rates of less than 25 percent. Nationally, only a little more than half of all college students graduate within six years—and all the people who start college but never graduate will earn substantially lower wages than those with degrees, which makes their student loan debt all the more burdensome. As for the students most in need, those from the bottom income quartile, only 31 percent who start college manage to complete a degree.

Forty-five percent of all those who did graduate in 2012 had jobs that did not require a degree, according to Federal Reserve data. Furthermore, the 2013 unemployment rate of recent college graduates exceeded that of the general population.

The costs of college rose as job opportunities at the margin have worsened. Although 30 percent of the adult population have college degrees, only 20 percent of jobs require college degrees, according to the Department of Labor. Moreover, those with some college but no degree now earn about as much as their high-school-educated peers. In fact, recent data suggest that the returns of "some college" have essentially fallen to zero.

Colleges have benefited from the huge increases in federal spending, as they have raised tuitions year after year at rates far outstripping inflation. But poor and working-class Americans certainly have *not* benefited. Just as the government spurred a housing bubble and induced poor people to take out mortgages they could not afford, federal student aid programs have caused unemployed or underemployed college graduates to take on crushing student loan debt. And the effective delinquency rate on student loans is now as high as it was on subprime mortgages at the height of the housing crisis.

Through the student loan program, the federal government and institutions of higher education effectively partner to maximize the number of young people becoming indebted tuition-paying students. The students end up holding all the debt, regardless of whether they graduated or pursued a course of study that qualified them for a decent job enabling them to repay the debt.

The explosion of federal financial-aid programs has done little to help poor people graduate from college. A smaller proportion of college graduates now come from low-income backgrounds than did so before federal financial-aid programs became so large. Only about 7 percent of recent college grads come from the bottom income quartile, compared with 12 percent in 1970.

According to the Educational Longitudinal Study, which followed high school sophomores from 2002 to 2012, only 14 percent of students from the lowest socio-economic quartile had attained a bachelor's degree or higher after ten years. Another study found that 5 percent of low-income eighth graders born in the 1960s earned a bachelor's degree, compared to just 9 percent of those born in the 1980s. That's only a four-percentage-point increase, despite the vast increase in student loan funding since 1980.

The federal student loan program is just another glaring example of how big government backfires. Government programs routinely fail to deliver on their promise to help the poor, the working class, and the otherwise vulnerable in our society. In fact, they too frequently end up hurting those the government expanders claim to help.

Bigger is better for those privileged groups who have the contacts, money, and power to leverage big government. For everyone else, big government often backfires.

Point #6

←——→

BIG GOVERNMENT CROWDS OUT CIVIL SOCIETY

"Government is simply the name we give to the things we choose to do together."

This line, typically attributed to former congressman Barney Frank, is a favorite of progressives when they call to expand government.

But the statement completely misrepresents the American experience. It ignores the fact that the non-governmental institutions of civil society—the family, schools, religious organizations, civic groups, neighborhood associations, and the rest—provide the cultural glue that makes political self-government possible. Civil society has always preceded and given rise to government, which was never intended to be the principal occupation of society.

The trouble is that as government becomes the dominant institution in society, it crowds out competing social institutions. The more things government does, the fewer things Americans are able to do together in other social venues.

Government is a necessary institution in democratic society, but it cannot take the place of all the other social institutions. A vibrant civil society requires a balanced ecosystem of interdependent institutions. When government attempts to replace or diminish other institutions, all of society falters, including government itself. It can be a vicious circle: government centralization weakens those social bonds formed through families, religion, communities, and civic organizations; and the weaker those nongovernmental institutions become, the more government steps into the void.

The fraying of civil society is particularly problematic for the "little guy" for whom the government expanders claim to work. That's because the institutions of civil society generally offer the most effective help to the common person who wishes to advance his or her life condition.

For the vast majority of people, life is lived parochially and locally, not nationally. Local communities and associations give shape and meaning to our lives, as we are embedded in an intricate web of human relationships, associations, and cultural mores. At the local level is where most of the meaningful things in life happen: raising a family, working at a job, starting a business, interacting in social groups, volunteering in the community. Global and

DID YOU KNOW?

Since the War on Poverty began, the percentage of men between the ages of twenty-five and thirty-four who dropped out of the workforce has quadrupled.

nationalized connections can become abstractions, whereas real civic self-government and genuine concern for others are possible in the communities in which people live. Because family, community, religion, social relationships, and work are crucial for meaningful living, the institutions of civil society promote human happiness more effectively than big-government programs can.

Civil society and its institutions also act as a buffer between the individual and the state, limiting the power of government. This is one reason why big-government advocates ignore the effects of their favored policies on civil society. Broadly speaking, they hold a negative view of society—as Yuval Levin of the Ethics and Public Policy Center put it in a 2013 speech, they "tend to begin from outrage at what is bad and broken and seek to uproot it," and government is their favored reform tool. Proponents of defined government, by contrast, see in society something positive that can help individuals elevate their lives—in Levin's words, they "tend to begin from gratitude for what is good and what works in our society and then strive to build on it."

Over the past several decades, the government expanders have won out. Civil society has been weakened considerably, and countless Americans have suffered for it.

A BUFFER BETWEEN THE INDIVIDUAL AND THE STATE

The nongovernmental institutions of civil society transmit to each new generation those virtues without which free societies cannot survive. When these institutions function properly, they help prevent people from becoming too dependent on government. They also unify people and empower them to control government.

When an expanding government crowds out civil society, all that connects diverse individuals in society is a rights-allocating government, with people having nothing in common other than a competitive struggle for government benefits and recognition. This struggle produces an adversarial culture that particularly hurts the poor, who need an assimilation culture that connects them to the rest of society.

In his book *The Fractured Republic*, Levin argues that many of our social problems reflect "a view of society as consisting only of individuals and a state," which has "set loose a scourge of loneliness and isolation." At the same time, Levin writes, the federal government "now engages in more direct intervention . . . in the daily lives of Americans than it ever has in peacetime." These two results—individual isolation and federal interventionism—are connected. The former occurs because the latter has weakened mediating institutions like churches and neighborhood organizations, which are powerful decentralizing forces that scatter economic, social, and political power too widely for any government to seize complete control of society.

Progressive elites claim that America's strength lies in its diversity, and that its greatest challenges lie in the toleration of that diversity. But this is not right. The reality of America is diversity, but its greatest strength has always been its ability to unify the diverse. This strength, however, can be maintained only by a culture of commonality, by a society that means more than just a large number of individuals ruled by a big central government. Of course, the diversity touted by progressive elites is not the genuine diversity that emerges from the pursuits and values of a free, pluralistic civil society; it is a diversity coerced through a federally managed adversarial culture that divides people into groups of victims and oppressors.

Religious organizations are institutions of civil society that greatly influence quality of life, especially for the poor. To religious institutions, which strive to practice the virtues of charity and compassion, the poor are not just clients or program beneficiaries—they are children of God. So the work of religious activists is guided not by the job descriptions of government bureaucrats but by a higher duty. Unfortunately, the crowding out of religion from the public square has deprived the poor of committed activists who focus on individualized needs.

The ACA's health-care mandates illustrate this crowding out. The law forced the Little Sisters of the Poor, an order of Catholic nuns that runs homes for the elderly poor, to violate their religious beliefs by having to offer contraceptive coverage for their employees. Until the U.S. Supreme Court unanimously overturned lower-court rulings, the Little Sisters faced $70 million in fines, which would have denied the elderly poor the compassionate care offered by the Little Sisters.

The fact that a private institution cited religious beliefs to oppose the program goals of a growing federal government seemed to incense federal officials to the point of vindictiveness. Even though the Obama administration let other organizations, like unions and congressional employees, escape the ACA's mandates, it went after the Little Sisters and their religious beliefs, which dared to intrude on the social space that the federal government now claimed for itself. The administration paid little heed to the fact that religious organizations and other nongovernmental groups provided health and welfare services long before the government got involved. The Little Sisters, for instance, have ministered to the poor and elderly since 1839. A century ago, religious organizations had a prominent presence in the nation's prisons. These organizations and their committed volunteers focused not on some generic bureaucratic blueprint but on the specific needs of the individual. But as the federal government expanded its role during the Great Society era, it monopolized social-welfare venues, such as prisons, and pushed out those private organizations.

WHERE GOVERNMENT CAN'T HELP

Poverty is not only material. Its most debilitating deficits are behavioral and social; its most serious deprivations are cultural. Poverty accompanies a living environment of chaos and harshness. Even if the poor get financial sustenance, they will continue to struggle if they lack social relationships or have no direction to their lives.

The unemployed poor suffer in ways that go beyond economic injury. They suffer from all the deprivations caused by a failure to work. There is dignity in earning a livelihood and providing for one's self and family. Work fosters virtues that can come from nowhere else—virtues like self-reliance, diligence, dependability, and personal responsibility. Correspondingly, unemployment can be demoralizing and dehumanizing.

Being poor today is not like being poor in 1936, during the depths of the Great Depression. The material poverty was much worse in 1936, but it did not have the generationally debilitating effect that poverty today is having. The poor in 1936 became the middle class in 1956. That is in large part because, in 1936, the larger culture supported the fundamental goals of life: to live dignified lives, to be law-abiding and hardworking, to be faithful to one's family, to uphold the ideals of decency. This cultural direction prevented the poor from falling into a pit of chaos, desperation, and dependence, out of which they or their children could not climb.

Materially, the situation for the poor has actually improved. According to data compiled by the Congressional Budget Office, the average after-tax household income for the poorest quintile of American households increased 30 percent between 1979 and 2010, from $14,800 to $19,200 (both numbers reported in 2010 dollars); the second-poorest quintile saw after-tax income rise 31 percent, from $29,900 to $39,100. Many people living at the lower economic levels of society have iPhones, computers, and flat-screen televisions. Still, inequality is getting worse, as the poor fall further behind and have a harder time entering the middle class. Their lives are in a downward spiral, as they are cut off from a culture of responsibility and self-discipline that government spending programs cannot create. So a vicious circle ensues: the more the federal government drains the energy and independence of the social mediating institutions, the more that individuals become increasingly atomized and separated; and the more individuals become disconnected, the more a centralized government steps into the void.

Government is inherently limited in its ability to fight poverty. Government spending cannot provide the poor with the social and cultural support systems that flourished generations ago. It cannot provide the social capital they need to improve their lives. This social capital includes such virtues as self-discipline, delayed gratification, ambition, and respect for authority. These virtues can be inculcated only through the institutions of civil society, which are more responsive to individualized needs than is government.

THOUGHTS ON BIG GOVERNMENT

"Government can help or hinder. But it is finally a task for the overlapping, plural associations of civic life in which citizens build and pass on those formative institutions—families, schools, churches, unions, and all the rest, including state and local governments—without which there is no democratic culture and, indeed, nothing for the federal government to either correct or curb or serve."

—Jean Bethke Elshtain, University of Chicago

As the social scientist James Q. Wilson demonstrated in *Two Nations*, family structure, not income, is the best indicator for all kinds of problematic behaviors, from delinquency to dropping out of school to out-of-wedlock pregnancy. There is no area of life in which children who grow up in broken or never-formed two-parent families do as well on average as children who grow up with both parents.

Government's inability to teach behavioral or cultural norms is evident in the field of job training. In 1962, Congress passed the Manpower Development and Training Act (MDTA) to provide training for workers who lost their jobs because of automation. A decade after MDTA's inception, the General Accounting Office reported that the MDTA was failing to teach valuable job skills and was more concerned with filling its program slots than with what trainees actually needed to learn.

Congress replaced the MDTA in 1973 with the Comprehensive Employment and Training Act (CETA). Despite tens of billions of dollars put into this program, it did a terrible job of training, focusing more on what the government agency wanted to do than what the individual trainees needed. An Urban Institute study concluded that participation in CETA programs resulted in "significant earnings losses for young men of all races and no significant effects for young women."

After CETA became a well-known failure, Congress replaced it with the Job Training Partnership Act (JTPA). This new program likewise failed. According to the Labor Department's inspector general, young trainees were twice as likely to rely on food stamps after JTPA involvement as before. In 1993 a Labor Department study showed that participation in JTPA "actually reduced the earnings of male out-of-school youths" by 10 percent.

So the federal government replaced the JTPA, too. In 1998, Congress passed the Workforce Investment Act (WIA).

That's four separate federal initiatives in a span of thirty-five years, all of which didn't help their intended beneficiaries and in fact hurt them.

These failures illustrate the point that a distant and impersonal federal government cannot change individual behavior or motivation and so cannot help people build better lives for themselves. The complexity of social ills plaguing low-income communities requires direct, hands-on intervention by civic organizations that can help people escape the forces holding them back. Government dependency, on the other hand, just continues the breakdown of civil society and families.

REJECTING CULTURAL VALUES

Eliminating the disciplining restraints of cultural values may sound appealing at first, but in reality that only works for the elite, because only the elite have the financial resources, educational background, and connections to go their own way. The elite do not need, or think they do not need, the strength of the family to protect them from economic storms. The elite do not think they need the guidance of religion to lead them to happy, fulfilled lives. The goal of the elite is to be freed from the inherited authorities of family, community, and religion, because those institutions may impose values that restrict the ability to experiment in lifestyles.

The lifestyle liberation promoted by the elite comes as a kind of trade-off for ways in which the government has restricted other types of freedom. Even though the political elite has greatly diminished economic freedom through the federal government's pervasive regulation, that elite has still tried to claim the freedom agenda by promoting cultural freedom or lifestyle liberation. But this cultural freedom has not worked well for the poor. Take state-sponsored gambling. It is sold as an exercise in personal freedom and a release from the traditional moral criticisms of gambling. And so the state subsidizes it, promotes it, and profits from it. And the wealthy and political elite praise it as an example of lifestyle liberation, because gambling produces substantial licensing and tax revenues—revenues that would otherwise have to be paid through income taxes on the wealthy. Instead, through gambling, it is the poor and working class who foot the bill for government.

As Christopher Lasch demonstrated in his 1996 book, *The Revolt of the Elites and the Betrayal of Democracy*, elites have spent decades attacking the moral, social, and religious underpinnings of the middle and working classes. Sixteen years later, Charles Murray documented the results of this elite campaign in his book *Coming Apart: The State of White America, 1960–2010*. Murray shows that elites have maintained their own social systems and supports, adhering to ideals like religion, marriage, industriousness, and honesty.

The problem, Murray says, is that elites are unwilling to "preach what they practice." The rich may still live in traditional marriage settings and participate in religious organizations, but they do not defend marriage or religion as foundational standards for the rest of society. In fact, they often denigrate traditional cultural values in public discourse. But they quietly (and selfishly) pass on those standards to their children in gated communities, while undermining the common civic culture and separating the lower classes from America's core cultural institutions.

As a result, Murray argues, we have seen for the first time "the emergence of classes that diverge on core behaviors and values." In a world increasingly dominated by big government, the lower classes have built their lives around the empty models of single parenting, rejection of religious belief, and social isolation.

Substituting values-void big government for the values-inculcating institutions of civil society has been nothing short of disastrous for the poor and working classes. Since the War on Poverty began, out-of-wedlock births have grown sixfold, and the percentage of men between the ages of twenty-five and thirty-four who have dropped out of the workforce has quadrupled, even though American men in that age group have never been healthier.

What has crippled the poor today is the disappearance of their social and cultural support systems. Economist Thomas Sowell has observed, "The black family survived centuries of slavery and generations of Jim Crow, but it disintegrated in the wake of the liberals' expansion of the welfare state." And the late senator Daniel Moynihan once wrote, "It cannot too often be stated that the issue of welfare is not what it costs those who provide it, but what it costs those who receive it."

THE TRUE COST OF BIG GOVERNMENT

Since the dramatic government expansion of the Great Society era, big-government advocates have tried unsuccessfully, and often destructively, to effect a massive economic redistribution toward the poor. But what these advocates have succeeded at is bringing about a moral and cultural redistribution away from the poor, thus further widening the inequalities in society.

The poor are falling further behind and having a harder time entering the middle class. This is because the social and cultural poverty of the current age has much more devastating consequences than just the economic poverty. In pushing out the values-inculcating institutions of civil society, big government has neutralized or even undermined the values on which these institutions rest. This has not produced a flowering of freedom. Instead, it has robbed working-class America of social capital. It has weakened families, gutted public education, increased out-of-wedlock births, turned neighbors into strangers, heightened crime, and produced a fragmented and isolated citizenry. Human freedom will further erode when government must pass even more laws and create even more bureaucratic programs to try to replace all the social guidance and support once provided by families, communities, schools, and religions.

It is no surprise that the incidents of corporate greed, financial misconduct, and unethical professional behavior are continually rising, despite the fact that more and more laws are passed to combat those occurrences. It is no surprise that child abuse and classroom violence and fatal interactions between police and individuals are escalating, despite all the government programs and education policies. What controlled and guided human behavior for centuries has been cast aside for big-government rules that command no allegiance. Big government has proved incapable of being a reliable moral compass.

Conclusion

◀━━━▶

CHANGING THE DEBATE

The debate over the size and scope of the federal government has not let up since the time of the New Deal. But, for the most part, that debate has been one-sided.

Champions of defined government have done little to stop the relentless growth of government, even when they have held political power. They seemed to achieve a major victory in 1996, when a Democratic president, Bill Clinton, declared, "The era of big government is over."

But that seems like ancient history now.

The government expanders have convinced a significant portion of the population that big government is the answer to every imaginable problem. As time goes on, the federal government seizes more power and absorbs more and more taxpayer dollars.

There are many reasons for the growth of government. But advocates of defined government often hurt their own cause. Whereas big-government advocates speak as if they have the best intentions of the common person at heart, proponents of defined government typically talk abstractly about rates of economic growth, about wasteful and inefficient programs, about constitutional provisions on limited government. Such arguments have legitimate foundations but miss the point. As American Enterprise Institute president Arthur C. Brooks put it, those who press the case purely in terms of statistics or efficiencies end up sounding like "tax accountants to billionaires."

But the real problem is that such arguments fail to counter the fundamental claim of big-government advocates: that big government provides vital support to the average American, who cannot get ahead in a society controlled by the wealthy and politically powerful.

The foundational argument underlying big government is a myth. Big government does not help the poor, the working class, and the middle class, even though those groups provide the justification for big government. In fact, big government often hurts the supposed beneficiaries of government largesse. Those who gain the most from big government are the elite and the powerful.

The myth of big government has been repeated so often that it has come to be taken as true. But any real concern for our fellow citizens requires that this myth be exposed.